Hermann Von Holst

The French revolution tested by Mirabeau's career; twelve lectures on the history of the French revolution, delivered at the Lowell institute, Boston, Mass.

Hermann Von Holst

The French revolution tested by Mirabeau's career; twelve lectures on the history of the French revolution, delivered at the Lowell Institute, Boston, Mass.

ISBN/EAN: 9783337229849

Printed in Europe, USA, Canada, Australia, Japan

Cover: Foto ©ninafisch / pixelio.de

More available books at **www.hansebooks.com**

THE FRENCH REVOLUTION

TESTED BY MIRABEAU'S CAREER

TWELVE LECTURES ON THE HISTORY OF THE FRENCH REVOLUTION, DELIVERED AT THE LOWELL INSTITUTE, BOSTON, MASS.

BY

H. VON HOLST

Vol. II.

CHICAGO
CALLAGHAN & COMPANY
1894

Dedicated

TO

MY WIFE,

ANNIE ISABELLE, née HATT,

IN TOKEN OF GRATITUDE

FOR THE SYMPATHY AND AID

GIVEN ME FOR TWENTY-TWO YEARS

IN MY LITERARY LABORS.

TABLE OF CONTENTS.
Vol. II.

LECTURE	PAGE
VII. "The Party of One Man"	1
VIII. The 5th and 6th of October, 1789, and the Memoir of the 15th	41
IX. The Decisive Defeat of the 7th of November	83
X. Other Defeats and Mischievous Victories	128
XI. Mirabeau and the Court	167
XII. The End. A Unique Tragedy	207

THE FRENCH REVOLUTION.

TESTED BY

THE CAREER OF MIRABEAU.

LECTURE VII.

The Party of One Man.

AT the solemn opening of the States-General, as we heard Mirabeau say, "they were drunk with the desire to applaud, and they applauded unto satiety." As to one man, however, the assembly made an exception. Gouverneur Morris, who was present, reports, that when Mirabeau entered, he was "hissed." The days came when he was more thunderingly applauded than any one else, but at the same time hissing never ceased, and it is still continued, I am tempted to say, not only in France, but by France. Not to applaud him is impossible, for it would only prove that one is too dull to understand that he was a genius. But it is with a kind of reluctance and a somewhat apologetic air that France glories in him, while the hissing is not done with regret. There is an undertone of elation in the moral satisfaction derived from it. It seems to say: "There is, of course, no denying that he was the greatest orator of the revolution, but don't insult me by supposing that this betrays me into not taking him at his true worth."

This applies also to his best biographer. Mr. Loménie once calls him "the inexplicable man."[1] Some historians might have hesitated to write and publish several stout volumes on a man, so long as they had to confess to themselves that they failed to understand him. Happily Mr. Loménie did not think so—happily, for he has brought many new facts to light and enabled us to see in many respects more clearly and more correctly. Mirabeau's biography, however, must needs still be written, for it evidently can only be written by a man who does understand him.

That Mr. Loménie did not succeed in this is, in my opinion, due to the following causes:—

[1] Œuvres., II. 436.

The historian has to be an uncompromising searcher for truth. In searching for truth he has, however, not to be animated by the spirit of the state attorney working up a case, but by that broad sympathy capable of seeing that, if men and times are but really *understood*, the moral *guilt* of their follies and crimes almost always appears diminished by one-half. Men, however, never can be really understood, if they are not judged as children of their times. I am far from charging Mr. Loménie with having overlooked this; but, I think, he has not allowed it all the weight that must be accorded to it. Much of what ought to be charged against the times—principally or, at least, to a considerable extent—is made to appear, altogether or chiefly, an item of Mirabeau's personal account. He is a genuine son of his times. Not only their characteristic brilliant traits, but their follies and vices also have in him a pre-eminent representative.

Mr. Loménie, besides, has not found his way out of the maze of contradictions presented by Mirabeau's character. He has not kept sufficiently in mind that almost all men are a compound of inconsistencies and self-contradictions. Truly harmonious and thoroughly consistent characters are so rare, that they might be called white ravens, but with most men—and especially uncommon men—there is one predominant trait, and this furnishes the key to the character. Mr. Loménie thinks he has discovered this predominant trait in Mirabeau's character, but having unconsciously approached his task with the spirit of the state attorney, he necessarily got into a wrong track, and every step led him further away from the correct solution of the problem. Mirabeau's policy, he asserts, " is, then as always, an essentially personal policy," directed by the " passions and calculations of personal interest." [1] It is true, so long as Mirabeau, to a great extent by his own fault, practically lives without any task, impure and unscrupulous egotism is indeed to a revolting degree the propelling force of his life. But the more ambition asserts itself as his dominant passion, the more also purer and higher motives contend for the mastery with this egotism; and when the revolution at last furnished him with a task worthy of his genius and adapted to his character, they are, in the main, to such a degree in the ascendant, that the charge only proves how utterly the biographer has, in fact, failed to understand his hero.

[1] Corresp., V. 318, 319.

Sure enough, Mirabeau writes himself on July 17, 1790, to La Marck: "If one has not more energy and does not dispose of more means, I shall soon be forced to a change of rôle without a change of will; for after all my strength is my existence, and in the general conflagration I must needs employ it for myself, if I find no way of applying it to the public welfare."[1] These lines, however, only apparently sustain Loménie's accusation. If properly read, they are a striking refutation of it. The declaration, that in future he will eventually be guided by his personal interests, manifestly implies the assertion that this has thus far not been the case; and this declaration is a warning, nay a threat, provoked by deep patriotic dismay, because the king had once more so pitiably failed to improve the opportunities offered three days before by the Federation festival. Besides, the emphasis is to be laid on the assurance, that his will is not to change. So long as he lived up to this promise, he could not fail to find some way to use his strength for the public welfare—if no longer to effect any positive good, at least to avert greater evils. The grain of truth, which Loménie's assertion contains also as to the

[1] Corresp., II. 102.

period of the revolution, is confined to the confession: "My strength is my existence." Though his despondency more than once became so great, that he professed to be longing and ready to abandon the field, he never could have done it. So long as things could become worse than they were, he had to stay in the thick of the battle. With him it could be ended only with his existence—and primarily, not because patriotism required this of him, but because his strength was his existence. His father was right, when he wrote as early as 1771 : " At bottom I am afraid, that to calm him down and to extinguish him would amount to pretty much the same thing."

As Mr. Loménie is satisfied that personal interest was the determining element in Mirabeau's policy, it goes without saying that he, like most Frenchmen, thinks his claim to greatness rests principally upon his eloquence. Unquestionably, as the miraculous lance is essential to the Achilles of the poet, so his oratorical pre-eminence is essential to the historic Mirabeau. But the oratorical powers of the Titan of the first period of the revolution, no more constitute this Titan than the lance of Achilles was Achilles.

Loménie feels himself that Mirabeau held an

absolutely unique position in the Assembly, and this was certainly not due to his being the greatest of its orators. Louis Blanc very felicitously characterizes this unique position. He closes the description of the three main party groups, which were gradually evolved in the Assembly by the political contest, with the graphic sentence: "The fourth party consisted of one man, Mirabeau."

Yes, and he not only *was* a party by himself, but he *knew* beforehand that it would be so, and was *determined*, that it should be so. He writes, in May, 1789: "It is to undertake a proud and difficult task to minister to the public welfare without sparing any party, without worshipping the idol of the day, without other arms than reason and truth, respecting them everywhere, respecting nothing but them, having no other friends than them, no other enemies than their adversaries, not recognizing another monarch than one's conscience, no other judge than time. Well! I shall perhaps succumb in this enterprise, but I shall persist in it."[1]

This being the lofty task he intends to assume,

[1] "*Mais je n'y reculerai pas.*" I think this implies more than only not to shrink from it.—Corresp., I. 349.

it could not be personal ambition alone that caused him to write to his father immediately after his arrival in Provence: "This will be my compass: I must be a member of the States-General." In a letter to Mauvillon [1] he states his other consideration with blunt directness: I have "the presumption to believe myself useful and even necessary to them." Necessary in the strict sense of the word, and he says with the same blunt directness why so. In his Note of June 20, 1790, he urges the queen to force Lafayette to conclude an alliance with him, by telling him: "M. de Mirabeau is the only statesman of this country; no one else has his *ensemble*, his courage and his character." [2] So it was. Many others were—in a high, and partly even in a higher degree than he —endowed with this or that quality of the statesman, but he alone was a statesman in the full sense of the word, for in him alone *all* the required qualities were combined, and of the most essential ones he was possessed in an eminent

---

[1] Sept. 22, 1788. Lettres à Mauvillon, 396.

[2] Corresp., II. 42. To Mauvillon he had written: "Quand vous aurez lu (the papers which he sends him), j'ose dire que votre estime redoublera, et que vous direz: *Voilà enfin un Français qui est né avec l'âme, la tête et le caractère d'homme public.*"—Lettres à Mauvillon, 462.

degree. Mr. Stephens hits the nail on the head in saying: "He was essentially a practical statesman, and that is the reason why his character is so little appreciated by Frenchmen."[1]

The first requirement of the practical statesman is fully to understand the situation, i. e., to base his calculations and his acts completely and exclusively upon the stern facts, and not upon what might be and ought to be. If the National Assembly and its successors were wanting in anything it was this, and if any one thing can be designated as the main root of the follies, crimes, and disasters of the revolution, it is this. Mirabeau did not need the painful lessons of experience to learn this truth, and to realize its overshadowing import. And if he could be justly charged with inconsistency in every other respect, unswerving and relentless consistency characterizes his political career in the application of this truth. Half a year before the States-General meet, he writes to Mauvillon: "Three roads must lead us to the most inalterable indulgence: the consciousness of our own shortcomings, the discretion which is afraid to be unjust, and the desire to do good, which, as it cannot recast either men or things, must try to

[1] Hist. of the Fr. Rev., I. 430.

derive advantage from all that is, as it is."[1] And ere the organization of the Assembly is effected, he rebukes Siéyès and warns the deputies of the third estate, saying: "There is this essential difference between the metaphysician, who, in the meditation of the study, grasps the truth in its energetic purity, and the statesman who has to take into account the antecedents, the difficulties, the obstacles; there is, I say, this difference between the instructor of the people and the political administrator, that the one thinks exclusively of *what is*, and the other occupies himself with what *can be*."[2]

Now what was the situation at the meeting of the States-General? Its determining features can be stated in three sentences. A revolution was not impending, but the country was in the midst of a revolution; in certain directions this revolution had to be radical, if the political and social

---

[1] Oct. 22, 1788. Lettres à Mauvillon, 416. In the same letter he says : " En vérité, dans un certain sens tout m'est bon ; les événemens, les hommes, les choses, les opinions ; tout a une anse, une prise. Je deviens trop vieux pour user mon reste de force à des guerres ; je veux la mettre à aider qui aident. . . N'excommunions personne et associons-nous à quiconque a un côté sociable. *Mal est ce qui nuit, bien est ce qui sert.* Nous devons nous garder d'être ennemis des autres écoles ; c'est la posterité qui marquera les rangs."

[2] Œuvres, I. 237.

regeneration of the commonwealth was to be effected; if proper measures were not taken at once, the revolution was sure to rush beyond the proper limits and thereby itself put its achievements into the greatest jeopardy. From the outset Mirabeau consciously plants his feet firmly and squarely upon these three basal facts.

As to the first, sufficient proof has already been adduced by some quotations I had to give in former lectures. In a few minutes I shall offer one more.

As to the second, he wrote, on the 16th of August, 1788, to Levrault:[1] "*War against the privileged classes and against privileges*, that is my device." And when, in January, 1789, a Paris paper called him "a mad dog, upon whom the *Provençaux* could not bestow the slightest confidence," he replied: "If I am a mad dog, that is an excellent reason to elect me, for despotism and privileges will die of my bite."[2] *His* revolutionary programme is comprised in these two sentences. He never extended it beyond them. But from the first it was perfectly clear to him that the revolution would be more than loth to stop there. Malouet, who is not subject to the suspi-

[1] Mémoires, V. 187–189.   [2] Ib., V. 269.

cion of being biased in his favor, testifies in his Memoirs: "He is perhaps the only one in the Assembly who has seen from the beginning the revolution in its true spirit—that of a total subversion." Indeed, from the beginning. More than four months before the meeting of the States-General, he wrote to the minister Montmorin:[1] "I, as citizen, tremble for the royal authority, which is more than ever necessary at the moment that it is at the verge of its ruin. Never was a crisis more embarrassing and presented more pretexts for license; never was a coalition of the privileged classes so menacing to the king, so dangerous to the nation; never did a national Assembly threaten to be so stormy as that which is going to decide the fate of the monarchy, and to which one comes with so much precipitation and mutual distrust."

Why he is determined to wage a war of extermination upon the privileges is distinctly stated in the before-mentioned letter to Levrault: "The privileges are useful against the kings, but they are detestable against the nations, and ours will never have any public spirit as long as it is not delivered of them. For this reason we ought

[1] Dec. 28, 1788. Corresp., I. 340.

to remain, and I, personally, shall be very monarchical.¹ Ah, forsooth, what would a republic be, composed of all the aristocracies that gnaw us? The abode of the most active tyranny."

And in the same letter he states, as succinctly, why he confines his revolutionary programme to a war of extermination upon the privileges and despotism. "Do not let us undertake too much. Concurrence (of the States-General) in regard to taxes and loans, civil liberty, periodical assemblies, those are three capital points which must be based upon an explicit declaration of national rights. The rest will come quick enough."

"Do not let us undertake too much!" In October, 1790, he writes: " Because the Assembly has got stuck fast by *doing too much*, it is crushed by the ruins it has heaped up." ² And in December

---

¹ Je vous suppli de m'engager envers M. de Montmorin (in soliciting his support to get Mirabeau elected to the States-General) à tout ce à quoi vous vous engageriez vous-même à ma place, et à rien de plus. Je puis promettre d'épargner l'individu (Necker). Je ne puis pas promettre de respecter ou ménager d'autres principes que les miens. Mais ce qui est très-vrai, et ce qu'on peut croire, c'est que je serais dans l'Assemblée nationale très-zélé monarchiste, parce que je sens profondément combien nous avons besoin de tuer le despotisme ministériel, et de relever l'autorité royale."—Mirabeau, Nov. 16, 1788, to the Duc de Lauzun.—Mémoires, V. 200.

² Corresp., I. 214.

of the same year: "The work (of the Assembly) in its entirety presents to the eyes of the observer only an inextricable chaos, in which the legislator has lost himself by doing too much."[1] But it did not take him until the fall of 1790 to see that the Assembly realized every day, more and more, what he, before the meeting of the States-General, perceived to be the greatest danger. From the first moment he was fully aware of it, and therefore from the first moment he threw himself with equal energy into the two antagonistic parts, which the circumstances compelled him to play to his last hour.

He was universally looked upon as the very impersonation of the fierce and implacable revolutionary spirit. And that he was—to the extent of his own revolutionary programme. Irrevocably he was resolved to carry this out at any cost, to break down at any risk every resistance to it, from whatever quarter it be offered, for not to do so was with him to renounce with full consciousness the regeneration of France and to abandon her to her fate. It was he who, on the 23d of June, after the *séance royale*, without any authority from his co-deputies, dared to speak in their name and tell

[1] Corresp., II. 443.

the master of ceremonies, that the order of the king would not be obeyed. Whether he did it in the exact words handed down by tradition is a very irrelevant question, of importance is only the incontestable fact, that he took the initiative and forced his colleagues to the alternative, either to cover themselves with inextinguishable shame by shrinking from the task they had sworn in the tennis court to fulfil, or to challenge the government and the conservatives of the upper orders to appeal to force. And when, in the beginning of July, the concentration of troops around Versailles and Paris indicates, that a new *coup d'état* is contemplated, it is again he that steps forward, moving an address to the king, not only praying, but also warning him to desist.

" Have they foreseen, the advisers of these measures, have they foreseen, what consequences they must have even for the safety of the throne? Have they studied in the history of all nations, how the revolutions have commenced, how they have been brought about? Have they observed by what a pernicious concatenation of circumstances, the most moderate minds are thrown out of the bounds of all moderation, and by what a terrible impulse an intoxicated people plunges into excesses, the first idea of which would have made it tremble?"[1] And with a lucidity, which ought to have carried conviction even to the dull intellect of Louis XVI., he states the reason why the crown would stake its very existence in an attempt to prevent the Assembly from carrying out his programme.

"How can the people fail to become agitated, if one awakens its apprehensions in regard to the only hope that is still left to it? Does it not know that, if we do not break its chains, we shall have rendered them heavier, we shall have riveted oppression, unshielded we shall have delivered our fellow-citizens to the pitiless rod of their enemies, we shall have increased the insolence of the triumph of those who rob and insult them?" So it unquestionably was; and therefore no choice was left to the Assembly. If the government once more threw the glove into its face, it had to pick it up and fight to the bitter end, or the people would put their heel upon it as upon the government.

That people, who were too obtuse or too much enwrapped in their passions to realize the force of these arguments, did not see that his left was

[1] Œuvres, I. 305.

reining in as strongly as his right vigorously applied the lash, can hardly astonish one. Still it was quite as patent. From the first hour, he sets himself with all his strength against everything that goes beyond his own programme.

Even his colleagues of the third estate apprehend that " he will ruin the public cause by excess of zeal;"[1] and it is *he* who keeps them down to the policy of " masterly inactivity." " The impetuosity of this incendiary," he writes, referring to himself, " has produced what?—The doing-nothing of the commoners who, if they had done anything before having a plan, accord, cohesion (*de l'ensemble*), harmony, would have got stuck fast at every step, become the laughing-stock of Europe, the scourge of the realm, impotent as to everything except to do harm."[2] Not for a moment does the idea enter his head, that the commoners should confine themselves to passive resistance, but he sees that everything would be lost by precipitation. " In a word," he concludes the sentence just quoted, " they would have left the government no resource but their dissolution." On the 18th of May, he presents both sides of the question with equal clearness.

[1] Lettres à Mauvillon, 462, *sq.*   [2] Corresp., 1. 349.

"Let us not encourage the intriguers, not expose the weak ones, not lead astray, not alarm public opinion, let us go ahead with provident circumspection, but let us go ahead."[1]

The government at once furnished him an opportunity, pointedly to call attention to the fact, that such "provident circumspection" implied the imperative necessity, not to identify the king with the government. With a view towards initiating, promoting, and directing the crystallization of the unconnected particles constituting the States-General, he undertook the publication of a paper, called *Etats Généraux*. Prompted by its hatred and fear of him, the government at once suppressed it. In a letter to his constituents he fiercely denounced the order. "After a deceitful, crafty toleration," he exclaims, "a cabinet, pretending to have the cause of the people at heart, has the hardihood to seal up our thoughts, to grant free-trade to lies, and to forbid as contraband the necessary export of truth."[2] But at the same time he says: "Everybody knows to-day, that such false measures proceed at the most from the cabinet; that the king has no part in them." As

[1] Œuvres, I. 191.
[2] 1re lettre du comte de Mirabeau à ses commettans, p. 5.

yet, the attitude of public opinion towards him was such, that the incident excited comparatively but little indignation, because it was he that had been struck. But, although he again and again repeated the warning, neither public opinion nor the Assembly ever learned to understand that, if France was to remain a monarchy, it was indispensable thus to distinguish between the king and the government.

When he, like the other deputies of the third estate, is of opinion that the time for action has come, he still insists, and even more emphatically than before, that one must proceed with painfully discreet circumspection. "All conciliatory means are exhausted," he says, on the 15th of June, "all conferences are at an end; we can only take decisive and perhaps extreme resolutions. . . Extreme! Oh, no, gentlemen, justice and truth are always in a wise medium; extreme resolutions are always but the last resources of despair; and who could reduce the French people to such a situation?"[1] "Our course," he says, "must be equally judicious, legal and graduated."[2]

Legal! The impetuous tribune, whom the father appropriately called "Monsieur l'Ouragan,"

[1] Œuvres, I. 222.   [2] Ib., I. 228.

Mr. Cyclone, pleads for legality, and he is in dead earnest about it. As the upper orders persist in refusing to join the third estate, he urges the deputies to proceed alone, but to remain scrupulously within the bounds of legality in constituting themselves. Therefore he entreats them: " Do not assume a name that frightens. Devise one that cannot be contested, which, milder and not less imposing in its plentitude, is adapted to all times, is susceptible of all the developments which the events will put within your reach."[1] Therefore he insists that, whatever name be chosen, the sanctions of the king cannot be dispensed with. Therefore he contends with all his might against the third estate alone, calling itself " National Assembly," before having been joined by the upper orders, for there is a tremendous force in names—this name ignores the existence of the upper orders, which is not merely a fact,[2] but also the law of the land—therefore its assumption at this juncture virtually subverts the existing legal order of things and passes with the ploughshare over it—by a purely revolutionary act it radically and by principle severs, in regard to questions of the greatest moment, the present and the future

[1] Œuvres, I. 227.   [2] Ib., I. 244

from the past. He suffered his first portentous defeat, not because the third estate intended to plunge into a radical revolution, but because he had spoken a language as unintelligible to most of the deputies as if it had been a foreign idiom.

When clergy and nobility, partly upon a direct order of the king, had joined the Assembly, this was considered irrefutable proof that he had seen spectres in broad daylight. His lips discovered a bitter drop in the sweet cup of universal rejoicing. "The 23d of June," he said, "has made upon this people—agitated and suffering—an impression the consequences of which I fear. Where the representatives of the nation saw only an error, the people believed to see a conscious purpose to attack their rights and powers."[1] When the urgent remonstrances against the concentration of troops were cast to the winds by the government, and Necker was dismissed, the people proved that Mirabeau had read their minds correctly. They rose in open rebellion, stormed the Bastille, and, after the victory, soiled their hands by a number of atrocious murders. Mirabeau bluntly told the government and its instigators, that they were "only harvesting the fruits of

[1] Œuvres, I. 263.

their own iniquities. One despises the people and wants it to be always mild, always impassible! No; here is a moral to be derived from these sad events; the injustice of the other classes towards the people lets it find justice even in its barbarism." But again with the same intrepidity he exposes also the other side of the picture to the light. "I make haste to say that the whole National Assembly has well felt that the continuation of this fearful dictatorship exposes public liberty as much as the plots of its enemies. *Society would soon be dissolved* if the multitude, getting accustomed to blood and disorder, would put itself above the magistrates and bid defiance to the authority of the laws; instead of marching towards liberty, the people would soon throw themselves into the abyss of servitude; for but too often danger causes men to rally round the flag of absolutism, and in the midst of anarchy even a despot appears a saviour."[1] The end of the story of the revolution gives no doubtful answer

[1] Œuvres, I. 349. A few weeks later he writes: "Qui ne le sait pas? le passage du mal au bien est souvent plus terrible que le mal lui-même: l'insubordination du peuple entraîne des excès affreux; en voulant adoucir ses maux, il les augmente; en refusant de payer, il s'appauvrit; en suspendant ses travaux, il prépare une nouvelle famine."—Courrier de Provence, No. 23, 3d to 5th of Aug., 1789.

to the question, whether he was right or not. Others were as deeply impressed by this side of the picture. After the brutal murder of Toulon and Berthier by the populace, Lally-Tollendal moved that the Assembly put a stop to the horrors by issuing a proclamation to the people. Mirabeau commenced his comments upon the motion with the enunciation of the weighty truth: "Small means would uselessly compromise the dignity of the Assembly."[1] It was but another formulation of Washington's well-known sententious remark : "Influence is not government."

One of the main causes of the disastrous development of the revolution was that the Assembly utterly failed to comprehend this all-important truism. Mirabeau never lost sight of it for a single moment, and he fully understood that the maintenance of a real and strong government was quite as much as a revolution, a *sine qua non*, for the regeneration of France. Therefore he opposed Lafayette's motion to *commence* the work of reconstruction by formulating a declaration of the rights of man. "The statesman," he says, "furnishes arms to the people only in teaching it to use them, for fear that in a first fit of

[1] Œuvres, I. 342.

intoxication it might rush into horrors, turn them against itself, and then cast them away with as much remorse as fright. Therefore it is absolutely necessary that a declaration of rights do not precede the constitution of which it is the basis, in order that the principles of liberty, accompanied by the laws which are to direct its exercise, be a benefit to the people and not a snare and a torment." [1] Again he was defeated, and again the course of events is one uninterrupted succession of stunning proofs that he was right, if ever a statesman was.

He was capable of looking beyond the day, and his eye pierced through the most dazzling and seductive appearances to the sober and harsh essence of things. Therefore he, who has sworn that privileges shall die of his bite, calls the famous night of the 4th of August, which at one stroke shattered feudalism in France, "an orgy." "There you have our Frenchmen," he says in bitter irony; "here they have been"—alluding to the discussion on the rights of man—"a whole month disputing over syllables, and in one night they subvert the whole old order of the monarchy." He was not recreant

[1] Courrier de Provence, No. 28.

to the faith he had professed for many years, but he reproved the Assembly for acting as if it thought the arduous work of the political and social reconstruction of a great state could be done to advantage in the spirit of a crowd of half-grown girls, carried away by a sudden paroxysm of enthusiasm. "If one had properly discussed the propositions," he writes to his uncle,[1] "one would have destroyed less, but susceptibilities would have been excited in a less degree; every party would have regained, by the fusion of minds, what it would have lost by sacrifices; one would at least have avoided the danger of crushing under a heap of ruins the nascent edifice of liberty."

There is in the utterances I have mentioned—and if time allowed I could add an almost infinite number of similar character—something that is common to all of them. He does not strive—and that is the second indispensable requirement for a true statesman—for what is in itself desirable, but confines himself to what will be, under the given circumstances, a real achievement, because it does not go beyond what is adapted to the times and the people. In other words: Mirabeau wants a

[1] Oct. 25, 1789. Mémoires, VI. 176-181.

revolution only so far, and in such a way, that it can and will result in a reform, and he fully understands that to determine what will constitute a genuine reform one has to ascertain not only what needs reforming, but also how far the capacity for reform goes. Whatever lies beyond the limits of this capacity, must necessarily work harm, though it be ever so unquestionably a reform if considered independently of the given circumstances.

Now we have seen what the *ancien régime* had made of the people. If this be kept in view, it is patent that the capacity for reform was, of necessity, as limited [1] as the need of it was boundless;

---

[1] It is this basal fact which so many people still fail to understand. The National Assembly could enact any laws, but its fiat could not render the people over night fit for the laws it enacted. Mirabeau writes: "Nous périrons par la partie honteuse des finances, nous et notre magnifique révolution, si nous ne nous résolvons pas à circonscrire rigoureusement ce que nous pouvons.... Cependant changez votre système d'impôts, et laissez à l'industrie et au commerce, abandonnés au régime de la liberté, à réparer les plaies de la fiscalités et à fournir des moyens de réconstituer et d'amortir votre dette, et vous verrez ce que deviendra en quinze ans votre empire français constitué. Je dis quinze ans, parce que rien ne prendra de véritable racine que par un bon système d'education publique, et certainement il faut au moins quinze ans pour planter des hommes nouveaux."—Lettres à Mauvillon, 504.

for, as Mirabeau said, "Liberty never was the fruit of a doctrine elaborated by philosophical deductions, but of every-day experience and the simple reasonings elicited by the facts." Therefore, whatever broke loose from the past in such a way as completely to cut the ligaments of historical continuity, went necessarily too far. This the revolution utterly failed to understand, and to Mirabeau this was from the outset a self-evident truth. "We are not savages," he said, "coming naked from the shores of the Orinoco to form a society. We are an old nation, and undoubtedly too old for our epoch. We have a pre-existing government, a pre-existing king, pre-existing prejudices. As far as possible one must adapt the things to the revolution and avoid abruptness of transition."[2] From the beginning this was the very basal idea of his policy. As early as the 16th of June, the day on which the third estate constituted itself as National Assembly, he writes to Mauvillon: "The fermentation is prodigious, and one is irritated that I am always with the moderates. . . It is certain that the nation is not mature. The excessive inexperience, the terrible derangement of the government have put the revolution

[1] Œuvres, II. 18.   [2] Ib., II. 148.

into a hot-house. It has gone beyond our aptitude and instruction. I conduct myself accordingly."[1]

There are, however, very different types of moderates. Not only in the Constituent, but also in the Legislative Assembly, and even in the Convention, the majority—measuring with the standard of the times—were moderates, and yet the greatest responsibility for the disasters of the revolution rests in a way upon them, because they were only moderates in a general kind of way and therefore ever liable to be completely swayed by the impulse of the moment, thereby themselves forging the fetters, with which the radical minority chained them to their chariot. Mirabeau's moderation bore no more resemblance to this kind of moderation than the granite rock resembles the quicksand. It rested upon a simple notion, which, with him, was an unshakable conviction. Whatever, according to the logic of facts, followed from these premises, implicitly imposed moderation upon him and, at the same time, fixed the limits of it, provided always that the superior consideration of carrying out his own revolutionary programme did not force him, against his will, tem-

[1] Loménie, IV. 280.

porarily and in regard to specific questions, to disregard its behests.

"When," he said, on the 7th of August, 1789, "the royal prerogative, that is to say, as I shall show in due time, the most precious possession of the people is discussed, one will see whether I know the extent of it. Ah, I defy beforehand the most respectable of my colleagues to surpass the religious respect in which I hold it."[1] Nothing is to make him swerve by a hair's-breadth from fulfilling to the letter his promise, that despotism and absolutism shall die from his bite; but nevertheless the *ceterum censeo* of the arch-revolutionist is, that the royal prerogative must be maintained, not only in form, but also in substance and as an all-permeating fact. For if anything is clear to him it is this, that, while the French people never can dispense with a strong government, they now stand more than ever in need of it, partly because everything is in a state of disintegration and dissolution, and partly because, more than by anything else, the issuing of the revolution in a reform is imperilled by the danger that all powers will be usurped by the National Assembly. In the great debate on the question, what name the deputies of

[1] Œuvres, I. 385.

the third estate should assume in constituting themselves, he replies to Thouret: "He answers to what I have said on the necessity of the royal approval, that he does not deem it necessary when the people have spoken. And I, gentlemen, believe the royal veto to such a degree necessary that I should rather live at Constantinople than in France, if he were not to have it; yes, I declare that I should know nothing more terrible than the sovereign aristocracy of six hundred persons, who could render themselves to-morrow irremovable, the day after to-morrow hereditary, and would end, as the aristocracies of all the countries of the world, by encroaching upon everything."[1] "Here," says Ludwig Hæusser, "the history of the Convention is written in three sentences." Indeed, the worst form of absolutism is that exercised by a numerous assembly claiming to be invested with the sovereignty of the people and, consequently, arrogating to itself all governmental powers, including the judicial, the executive, and the constituent. This holds good for all times and all peoples. And in France it had necessarily to come to this, unless the royal prerogative was maintained, for according to the whole historical

[1] Œuvres, I. 242.

evolution, and according to the habits and customs of the people, which are a stronger force than even the law, there was for the time being but the alternative: either to have no strong government, or to let it rest with the king.

That is the reason why Mirabeau was determined from the outset to be " very monarchical," and why he unflinchingly stuck to this resolution to the last. He was simply in an eminent degree possessed also of the third indispensable quality of the true statesman: he understands that only what can be effected with the means already existing or capable of being created is attainable. Therefore he sees his task in ascertaining what these are and making the best of them, without stopping to ask whether they are what he would like them to be, or starting with laying down a policy at the risk of finding out, when it is too late, that it cannot be carried out, because the means required for it are not procurable. " One must accommodate oneself to the circumstances, and use the instruments which fate has given us,"[1] he said on the 15th of June.

Of all the circumstances by far the most important, however, was that, if left to itself, this

[1] Œuvres, I. 224.

Assembly would inevitably drift under the propelling influences of the other circumstances into such a condition that, as he said on the 27th of June,[1] "the representatives of the nation would no more be the masters of their movements ... and would be reduced to the worst of all calamities, that of having only the choice between mistakes," until they finally became "a legislative body ... which does everything, except what it ought to do."

There was only one way to prevent this: the government had to take the lead. This also was perfectly clear to Mirabeau even before the States-General met. In the remarkable letter of December 28, 1788, to Montmorin, which I quoted before, he says: "Does the cabinet, which has rushed into this fatal defile by trying to postpone the convening of the States-General instead of getting ready for them, occupy itself with the means how not to have to fear their control, or rather to render their co-operation useful? Has it a fixed and solid plan, which the representatives of the nation would only have to sanction?

"Well, I have this plan, Count. It is connected with that of a constitution which would save us

[1] Œuvres, I. 266.

from the plots of the aristocracy, from the excesses of democracy, from the profound anarchy, into which the government, by wanting to be absolute, has plunged with us." [1]

Impudent fool! He, upon whose garments the dust and mould of half the state prisons lay thick, daring to volunteer his advice to the government! He had the effrontery to renew the attempt, [2] when the States-General had met, requesting Malouet to act as mediator between him and the ministers. Malouet thus tells the story of his interview with him. "I distrusted him as much as I was prejudiced against him. I thought him one of the most dangerous innovators, and therefore I was very much astonished by his *début* with me. 'I have desired an interview with you,' he said, 'because I see that with all your moderation you are a friend of liberty, and because I am, perhaps even more than you, alarmed by the fermentation I see in the heads, and by the calamities to which it may lead. I am not the man to sell myself ignominiously to despotism; I want a free, but monarchical constitution, I do not want to undermine the monarchy, and if measures be not taken betimes, I see so many giddy heads in this Assem-

[1] Corresp., I. 341.   [2] In the last days of May.

bly, so much inexperience and exaltation, and in the privileged orders such inconsiderate acrimony and resistance, that I apprehend, with you, terrible commotions. I appeal to your uprightness; you are in touch with Necker and Montmorin, you must know what their intentions are and whether they have any programme at all. If this programme is sensible, I shall defend it." Montmorin peremptorily declined to see him, Necker reluctantly consented, but received him with haughty rigidity, as if the count was a lackey, obsequiously soliciting to be taken into the service of the gracious lord. That was just the right tone to assume towards a Mirabeau. A cutting remark, turning on his heel and leaving the room was the work of a minute. Mirabeau told Malouet: "Your man is a dunce; he shall yet hear from me."

We do not know the details of the plan, which the ministers refused to receive, but the leading idea of it is clearly indicated in the letter to Montmorin, and his subsequent speeches and writings are a running commentary upon it. The government, which has already virtually renounced absolutism by convening the States-General, shall unite with them in destroying the privileges and establishing a moderately liberal constitutional monarchy, governed in every respect by law, and only by law. " This coalition between the executive and legislative power, without which a state like France cannot last, without which an ever stormy liberty leaves only the alternative between despotism and anarchy." [1] That he repeats again and again in innumerable variations. Upon this unquestionably everything ultimately depended. But no more hopeless task could be conceived than to make either the people, the Assembly, or the court understand just this. As to the two former he says: " There is no power that does not go too far, when it throws off oppression and dictates the law after the victory. In the heat of discontent one hardly thinks that one can give sufficient extent to one's means and erect enough barriers against one's adversaries, and at the return of the calm one perceives that one has been betrayed into imprudence by fear." [2] And: " Victim of the evil, the nation has only been struck by the necessity of preventing its return; and its representatives, in the midst of the crisis, have taken

---

[1] Corresp., I. 380.
[2] Nouveau coup d'œil sur la sanction royale.—Mémoires, VI. 435.

all at once all the measures suggested to them by a too just resentment, and one experience which was not counterbalanced by any other."[1] He, however, through all mutations, held immovably aloft as the banner around which all true patriots must rally to avert utter ruin, the principle of an honest and close alliance between the executive and the legislative powers."

No mean courage was required to do this, for every day the people and the Assembly more implicitly recognized as an axiomatic truth which only irredeemable fools and conscious knaves could contest, Mably's doctrine: "Every legislator must start from the principle that the executive power has been, is, and will be unto eternity the enemy of the legislative power." If so, then Mirabeau, as nobody could take him for a fool, evidently was a conscious knave and a traitor in addition, and more than one gory head told what fate might be in store for a man on whose forehead the populace was made to see this double brand. More than once Mirabeau was told that his past services to the revolution only rendered his crime more unpardonable, and not a few considered it a crime in the fullest sense of the word, because he did not

[1] Ib., Mémoires, VI. 434.

confine himself to preaching the alliance between the two powers as the correct doctrine, but insisted upon its being consistently applied and even dared, when its proper application seemed to him to require it, to champion openly the executive against the legislative. Marat demanded that the highest among all the gallows, which he wanted to have erected, be assigned to the " accursed " Mirabeau. But if he was not the man " to sell himself ignominiously to despotism," he was no more the man to be cowed ignominiously by the clamoring of the populace and its demagogical leaders. If there was a man in the Assembly who was possessed of the fourth indispensable quality of the true statesman, courage, then it was he. He himself repeatedly and emphatically asserts it,[1] and his father fully endorses him in this respect. " Since Cæsar," as his father wrote in 1782, "there never was such audacity and temerity." One scene will suffice to show whether there was truth in the assertion. He is stubbornly contending for the royal prerogative in regard to the right of peace and war. The enraged Jacobins

---

[1] On the 24th of April, 1789, he writes to Montmorin: " D'aucun mortel, en dignité ou nom, la menace envers moi ne peut avoir ni grâce, ni convenance."—Corresp., I. 347.

are determined to carry their point at whatever cost. A vast excited crowd is collected before the hall of the Assembly, listening eagerly to the reading of an article bearing the significant title: "The great treason of Count Mirabeau disclosed." Two sentences will abundantly characterize it. "Take care that the people do not pour gold, the burning nectar, into thy viper's gullet to quench forever the thirst for it which consumes thee; take care that the people do not carry thy head in procession as that of Toulon, whose mouth they filled with hay." When he enters the Assembly, a friend warns him of the danger and shows him the article. He replies: "One will carry me away from here triumphant or in shreds," delivers one of his greatest speeches and conquers in the main.

Neither the Assembly nor the populace can make him wince. But he has not only the animal courage, which braves physical danger. Highly as he prizes popularity, not only for its own sake, but above all because it is power, he does not flinch before unpopularity either. "I did not need this lesson," he says in the speech just mentioned, "that it is but a small distance from the capitol to the Tarpeian rock. But the man who contends for reason, for his country, does not so easily acknowledge himself vanquished; who is conscious of having rendered good service to his country and principally to be still useful to it, who is not satiated by vain renown, and, compared to true glory, holds the success of a day in contempt; who is intent upon telling the truth, who wants to effect the public welfare independently of the ever vacillating opinions of the masses, finds in himself the reward of his services, the charm of his troubles, the price of his dangers; he may expect his harvest, his fate, the only one that is of interest to him, the fate of his name, only from time, the incorruptible judge, who does justice to all. Let . . . them abandon to the fury of the deceived people him who for twenty years wages war upon every oppression, and who spoke to the people of France of liberty, constitution, resistance, at the time when these vile calumniators lived in all the prevailing prejudices. What do I care? Such blows, dealt by such hands,[1] will not check my course. I tell them, answer, if you are able; then calumniate as much as you like."[2]

I ask, does a man, whose policy is always determined by essentially personal interests, speak and

[1] "*Ces coups de bas en haut.*"   [2] Œuvres, III. 356, 357.

act thus in such a situation? I ask, does he on this occasion merely brave physical danger and cast popularity to the winds, or must what he says and what he does be acknowledged to be a magnificent display of that highest courage of the true statesman, to take the initiative and assume responsibility? And his whole course in the National Assembly, from beginning to end, is one continuous string of manifestations of this greatest and most indispensable quality of the true statesman. Ah indeed, he must be hard of hearing, who cannot discern throughout this course the ring of the proud and stern declaration with which he announced his intention to go himself to rebellious Marseilles: "Marseilles will submit, or I shall perish!"[1]

[1] Corresp., II. 413.

LECTURE VIII.

The 5th and 6th of October and the Memoir of the 15th.

"*Consummatum est,* all is consummated... We can tell the National Assembly: Now you have no more enemies, no opponents, no *veto* to fear; you have but to govern France, to render her happy, and to give her such laws that the nations, following our example, shall make haste to transplant them and to make them flourish with them."[1] Thus Camille Desmoulins and the other statesmen of the Palais Royal judged the 5th and the 6th of October. The revolutionary storm had run its race. The goal was reached; the sky swept clean of all clouds. Henceforth the sun of liberty would shed its glorious light in dazzling effulgence on a peaceful and happy country.

If so, the millennium verily had come, when

[1] Révolutions de France et de Brabant, No. 1.

figs shall be gathered from thistles and the briar bushes bend low with the weight of grapes. "*Consummatum est.*" Ah, yes, there was but too much truth in these first two words. But what was consummated? The correct answer to this question must be found in the true story of those two portentous days, unless France was exempt from the law, that no less in the moral than in the physical order of things the fruit corresponds to the seed.

On the 14th of July the nobodies of Paris had learned to know their strength. They had acted an independent and decisive part, relegated the National Assembly to the second place, and put, with crushing effect, their heel upon the neck of the old government and the partisans of the past. Under the *ancien régime* the government had monopolized all political power, arrogating to itself the rôle of irresponsible political providence; from the storming of the Bastille it ceased—not legally, but in fact—to be at all a determining political factor, while public opinion held it ever more and more exclusively responsible for all real and supposed grievances. The authority of the National Assembly had apparently suffered no detriment from its having played but a secondary and, in the main, even only passive part in the catastrophe overwhelming the government on that decisive day. On the contrary. In the provinces, public opinion was practically unanimous in sustaining the Assembly as the legal enunciation of the nation's sovereign will. And between Paris and the Assembly there was seemingly no antagonism, because the Assembly had strongly disapproved of the policy, which Paris had forced the government to retract. They were virtually in accord as to the What, though their disagreement as to the How might be in truth somewhat greater than the Assembly cared to acknowledge after the accomplished fact. Paris had not merely acted as the arm striving, though not directly bidden by the head, yet in conformity with its will; but, having acted upon a sudden impulse, it did not at once fully realize to what an extent it had really emancipated itself from the National Assembly, and as yet it was not in the least consciously tempted to supersede the legitimate head, or even to usurp the character of a rival or co-ordinate head. According to all appearances, therefore, the 14th of July had inured altogether to the benefit of the Assembly. The government having been compelled to surrender at discretion, and there being no other rival power, it held uncontested and absolute sway over the whole country. Nor was there now any reason to let the nobodies of the capital have it all their own way again, in case they should try once more to lead in the dance as they saw fit. On the 14th of July they had had to deal only with half-hearted bungling "minions of despotism," commanding troops upon whom there was no reliance in such a fight. Now the substantial classes of the population, whose personal interests were at stake in an attempt to subvert law and order, were perfectly organized and well-armed. Surely, the National Assembly and the nation might rely upon the national guard to nip in the bud any serious danger eventually arising from that quarter.

There were many flaws in this reasoning, and soon but little perspicacity was required to discern them. At the beginning of August feudalism was broken down by the National Assembly, and before the end of the month the first attempt was made to do open violence to it. The marquis St. Huruge started at the head of a mob for Versailles, to bring the obnoxious representatives of the right to their senses by the application of the lynch-law cure.¹ Though he was foiled in such a way as to render him ridiculous and contemptible, the vista into the future was none the less ominously dark. What had failed now might succeed the next time. The essential fact was, that France had been notified not merely by empty words, but by a deed, that her regeneration was not to be left exclusively to the National Assembly. The Palais Royal was going to lend it a helping hand in the arduous task, and it considered it its incontestable right, as well as its patriotic duty, to do so whenever and howsoever it should deem meet. One lived and learned fearfully fast in those days. By this time the revolutionary catechism of the spokesmen of the Palais Royal was already reduced to the simple maxim: Whatever love of liberty and ardent patriotism dictate is manifestly paramount duty, and every duty presupposes the right to do what it bids one do. Their followers were fully equal to

¹ The resolutions passed at the *Café* Foy, of which I shall soon have to speak in another connection, very ingeniously reconciled the recourse to this infallible remedy with a commendable respect for the law: "Les citoyens réunis au Palais Royal pensent que l'on doit révoquer les députés ignorans, corrompus et suspects.

"La personne d'un député étant inviolable et sacrée, leur procès sera fait après leur révocation."

St. Huruge went to execute these resolutions.

this logic and their belief in the self-evident dogma was more honest than that of many of their leaders. As to them, therefore, Mirabeau certainly preached to deaf ears, when he wrote: "The success of the project would have been a thousand times more disastrous than the dissolution of the Assembly by a stroke of despotism. . . . The Assembly dissolved by citizens! dispersed by a faction! A civil war and a sea of blood would have been the least terrible of the consequences. The constitution was about to perish before being born . . . . you promise victims to popular fury, outrages to justice, blood and cruelties to the fatherland. Poor madmen! what more could you do if you were its enemies? . . . All the strength of the National Assembly is in its liberty; liberty resides in the combat of opinions. If there the opinions should be enslaved, the nation would be reduced to bondage. . . Your club is not France, and France would, after all, rather receive laws from her king than obey the National Assembly subjected to your threats and the docile instrument of your sovereign pleasure." [1]

There is an undertone of anxious misgiving bordering upon despair in the impassionate solem-

[1] Courrier de Provence, No. 34; Aug. 30, 1789.

nity of this adjuration, and yet the last sentence was too optimistic. If France were now forced to the alternative he indicated, and if it were done in such a way that the plainest mind could not fail correctly to understand the issue, she would unquestionably choose as he thought. But would she do so, in case it was done gradually and so as to obscure more or less the true issue? And supposing that even then her inclinations should prompt her to make the same choice, would she know how to assert her will? Would she still be able to do so? But howsoever the future might answer these questions, his main assertion was irrefutable: France will have exchanged the absolutism of the *ancien régime* for a worse despotism, if the self-appointed avengers of liberty of the capital be allowed to speak the decisive word. They scuttle the ship ere it is fairly launched.

On the 5th of October they knocked the bottom out of it, in a somewhat different manner from that intended by St. Huruge and his prompters and backers, but even more effectively.

According to the revolutionary legend the poorer classes of Paris were reduced to a condition verging upon famine. That is a gross exaggeration. The situation was sufficiently serious to throw the masses into a state of unrest and keep them excited without the aid of designing agitators. But this spontaneous fermentation was due much more to the apprehension of future distress than to the actual suffering of want. Bread was scarce, but thus far there had always been yet enough of it to keep maddening hunger from the door. In politically quiet times the public peace would not have been disturbed. But now all the demagogues needed to do to make the smouldering coals blaze up in a fierce flame was to let in a little air. The government helped them by daring to call into question the wisdom of some of the provisions of the laws framed by the National Assembly in pursuance of the resolutions of August 4th. The court, as usual, did the best to work the destruction of what it wanted to preserve. The mines, which blew up the foundations of the old order of things on the 23d of June and the 14th of July, had been dug and charged by itself. Now it furnished, by an utterly insane, because wholly purposeless demonstration, the fuse to the demagogues to blast their mine.

On the first of October the officers of the gardes-du-corps gave a banquet to the officers of the regiment of Flanders in the theatre of the royal palace at Versailles. Under the influence of the liberal potations many a bold sarcasm and denunciation was launched against the National Assembly and the revolution in general. Court ladies stimulated the royalistic enthusiasm of the valiant knights by decorating them with white cockades—white being the color of the Bourbons. The assertion, that cockades in the three colors adopted by the revolution [1] were insultingly torn off, was a malicious invention of the revolutionists. It could not be done, because no such cockades were in the room.

The time was certainly well chosen to indulge in such aimless provocations, for Loustalot had just proclaimed in his *Révolutions de Paris:* "A second revolutionary onset is needed; everything is getting ready for it."

When he wrote those words it was not wholly inconsistent with the facts to put the second half of the sentence into the impersonal form. This was completely changed by the banquet. The provocation was after all not demonstrative enough to cause a spontaneous uprising of the masses. But those who, for one reason or another, wished a second revolutionary onset, saw the excellent op-

[1] Strictly speaking they were as yet only the colors adopted by revolutionary Paris.

portunity it afforded them, their number was considerable, and among them was one man who had the means, when he chose to engage in operations of this kind, to do it on a large scale. From the first there is system and purposeful direction in the agitation. The masses seem to have been slower to warm up to the proper temperature than one had expected. To quicken the flow of their blood they had to be told that that of every true patriot was boiling. It is significant that the weekly papers had to tell of many dramatic and exciting occurrences, of which no mention whatever is made in the dailies. The suspicion is naturally awakened that the stirring stories are partly the product of the fertile editorial brain, or that at least gnats are made to do service as elephants, in order to " fire " the heart of the unsophisticated patriots. Enough conscious lying has been done in the revolution to keep the furnaces of hell aglow for many a year,[1] and the story of this banquet has come in for its due share. The alleged outrage upon the revolutionary cockade received a proper setting by a sinister tale of a treacherous plot

[1] Cam. Desmoulins frankly confessed : " La fable aida un soulèvement général aussi bien que la vérité, et la terreur et les ouï dire aussi bien que les faits notoires."—Révolutions de France et de Brabant, IV. 362.

hatched and about to be carried out by the court party. The king, it was asserted, was to be brought to Metz for the purpose of calling the partisans of the *ancien régime* to arms and setting France ablaze with the torch of civil war. In this story also there was a grain of truth. There were persons urging the king to yield no more, but to offer resistance to further encroachments of the revolution, and, in order to be able to do so, to get out of the centre of the storm and to go to the eastern frontier. Louis XVI., however, was far from lending a willing ear to these counsellors. On the evening of the 5th, when the women were already for hours in possession of Versailles, he still declared in a letter to Count d'Estaing that he would not fly, because to do so would be to inaugurate civil war; he even declined to do anything that might be interpreted as an intention to defend himself.[1]

[1] "Vous voulez... que je prenne un parti violent: que j'emploie une légitime defense, ou que je m'éloigne de Versailles... La fuite me perdrait totalement, et la guerre civile en serait le résultat... Dieu veuille que la tranquillité publique soit rétablie; mais point d'agression, point de mouvement qui puisse laisser croire que je songe à me venger, même à me défendre."—Correspondance inédite, I. 159, quoted by Buchez et Roux, Histoire parlementaire de la Révolution française, III. 111.

Resentful suspicion and fear were strong levers to work upon the imagination and the feelings of the masses, but the banquet furnished still another of even much greater power. " While the people are starving, the myrmidons of despotism spin treason, gorging themselves at Lucullian orgies!" That was a crushing argument in the ears of excited under-fed masses, fearing soon to see the wolf at their doors. And to persuade them that it was high time for them once more to act, was all that was needed. If they could be goaded into taking matters into their own hands, they were also sure to do what they were wanted to do. According to their reasoning, it was self-evident that to get the king to Paris was in itself an infallible and lasting cure of their grievances. The plotting aristocrats would be left out in the cold, and the king, whether he liked it or not, would have to do what they wished to be done. That he would be able to do it, was not subject to any question. The notion of the omnipotence of government, bred by the *ancien régime*, had not been eradicated by the revolution; it had, on the contrary, cast deeper root. It was not a pleasantry, when the king upon his forced entrance into Paris was jubilantly hailed as the " baker ;" these children of all ages were fully satisfied that they had now secured the baker, at whose bidding the bins had always to stay filled with flour and the ovens full of loaves.

The *Mercure de France* of September 5th reports, that already, on the 30th of August, they spoke at the Palais Royal "of bringing the king and the dauphin to Paris. All virtuous citizens, all incorruptible patriots were exhorted to start forthwith for Versailles."[1] So the first attempt to effect, by mob violence, the transfer of the royal residence to Paris antedated the realization of the idea by fully five weeks. Now, however, the prompters of the masses, as it seems, kept their ulterior purpose more in the background. It is true, Camille Desmoulins states, that on the evening of October 4th—a Sunday—" the women" agreed " to meet the following morning at the foot of the lantern to go from there to Versailles."[2] he wrote his narrative nearly a year after the October events. But that is no reason to doubt its

---

[1] Quoted by Taine, La Révolution, I. 127. The two projects of expelling the obnoxious deputies and of bringing the king to Paris, " pour y demeurer en sûreté au milieu des fidèles Parisiens," were combined in the motion discussed and adopted by this meeting in the famous *Café* Foy.—See Moniteur, I. 399, 417. The king was to be " requested."

[2] Révolutions de France et de Brabant, III. 365.

correctness in this particular. He cannot be suspected of having indulged in an invention, because it could serve no conceivable purpose; there were few men in Paris, if any, in a better situation to be well informed about a fact of this kind, and it was of a character so to impress itself upon the mind, that his memory could not fail him after so short a time. The letter, however, with which the municipal council sent a delegate at about noon, on October 5th, to the National Assembly and the ministers declared: "The representatives know of no other pretext for this revolt than the sudden fermentation caused by cockades in colors different from those of the Hôtel de Ville, a fermentation which the fear of lacking bread has rendered more dangerous."[1] It has been inferred, from the wording of this declaration, that at this hour the council was still ignorant of any intention to make an exodus to Versailles for the purpose of bringing the king to Paris. If this be correct, the council can hardly have been informed of the agreement made the evening before by the women. That they would have known of it, if secrecy had not been enjoined upon those who

[1] Procès verbal de la Commune, lundi, 5 octobre. Buchez et Roux, III. 120.

were parties to it, is, however, all the more certain, because the councilmen had just proved by some extraordinary measures that their eyes were widely open to the danger of a move in that direction.[1] The objection, that the fairies of the rear streets, garrets, and cellars were not likely to plan such a movement in secret, has no weight. The scheme did not originate with them; they were mere tools, and it was sufficient to instruct a comparatively small number of leaders. There is abundant evidence that the 5th of October was not a spontaneous revolutionary upheaval, but a well-laid plot. The official minutes of the council say: "It seems that the people have made the insurrection at the same time in the different quarters of the city, and that this insurrection was premeditated."[2]

At dawn the women commenced marching to the Hôtel de Ville. "On the way," says Camille Desmoulins, "they recruit among their sex travel-

[1] Loustalot reports, in the above quoted number of the *Révolutions de Paris:* "Dès le même soir, les représentans de la commune répandirent dans les districts qu'il y aurait à craindre que le peuple ne se portât, la nuit, dans les corps-de-garde pour désarmer la garde nationale, afin de partir aussitôt pour Versailles : on doubla les postes, les patrouilles, et la nuit se passa tranquillement."
[2] Buchez et Roux, III. 122.

ling companions as one recruits sailors in London: women are pressed into service." At the *Place de Grève*, "these women begin to let down the lantern religiously, as in great calamities the reliquary of Sainte-Geneviève is let down." Ere the guillotine became the centre-piece in the coat-of-arms of French liberty, the lanterns served the people as ever-ready gallows. The letting down of the lantern, therefore, was a most emphatic announcement that serious business was intended.

The gallows put into proper trim, the women tried to penetrate into the Hôtel de Ville. Lafayette, writes Camille, "was advised of this movement; he knew that all insurrections were commenced by women, whose maternal bosom is respected by the bayonets of the satellites of despotism." You see, there is no lack of cool and shrewd reflection in these revolutionary fire-eaters. When Camille takes the witness-stand in regard to such a fact, he can hardly be challenged, and according to him the women did not lead to quite the extent they are generally supposed to have done. The men used them as an impenetrable shield. Quite an ingenious idea! But is a charge with the bayonet the only way in which a large armed force can disperse a crowd of women? Was it lack of judgment, lack of skill, or lack of will, that prevented the general, who was "advised of the movement," to act while the mob could have been easily scattered to the four winds without shedding one drop of blood? Upon the unpaid national guard he could implicitly rely. The rioters knew it well. It was believed that it had been contemplated to disarm them by a sudden night attack upon their guard-rooms, and Loustalot states, that "the people relied more upon the fidelity of the paid" national guard.[1] His great astonishment at this most significant fact is wholly feigned. The paid national guard consisted of former soldiers of the regiment that had set the example of riotous insubordination, and of other elements that were, if not exactly riff-raff, at least first and second cousins of riff-raff. They were natural allies of the mob, and the 5th of October was entirely a day of the mob instigated by self-seeking demagogues. The unpaid national guard

---

[1] " Ce qui est incroyable, c'est que le peuple comptait plus sur la fidélité de la troupe soldée que sur celle de la troupe non soldée : problème étrange, et qu'on ne peut expliquer que par la foule d'inconséquences et de vexations que se sont permises et les comités des districts et les commandans de patrouilles."

consisted of the *bourgeoisie*, and the *bourgeoisie* was a perfect stranger to the plot. As yet the conditions were such, that it was only the fault of the man if he could not find in this the necessary strength to frustrate it.

Not many persons who have cut a prominent figure in great times, have lost so much by having the search-light of critical history turned upon them as Lafayette. As to the part he played on the 5th of October, he himself has always seen a halo around his head. But even the most favorable interpretation of it at all compatible with the hard facts, turns the streaming light of this halo into very dingy yellow. He seems to be quite unconscious that there are not only sins of commission, but also of omission. Yes, *sins* of omission. He was the responsible guardian of the public peace. Therefore it was his bounden duty to act at once and in such a manner, that a riotous demonstration of some hundreds of women could not develop into an irresistible uprising. He, however, practically remained a passive looker-on, *i. e.*, wasted hour after hour in fine speeches and unavailing entreaties, until, as he himself told the king, " the will of an immense crowd *commanded* the armed force and there was no possibility of preventing their going to Versailles."¹ Camille does him only justice in calling him "Temporizer Fabius." But he almost seems to suspect him of having rather willingly allowed the mob all the time it needed to become irresistible.² The famous white charger remained hitched to the post till the vanguard of women had arrived at Versailles; he mounts it at last, forced by the former *gardes françaises*, one of them telling him —accompanying the words with a suggestive gesture with his musket—" General, to Versailles or to the lantern!"³ and then he rides at such a pace that it is pretended, as Camille says with mocking exaggeration, the great horse needed nine hours for the journey.

¹ Report of the commission of the municipal council.
² Lafayette himself admits: "J'avais pensé depuis longtemps que l'assemblée serait plus tranquille et le roi plus en sureté à Paris."—Mém. de Lafayette, I. 286; édit. 1837-39. It is rather striking that, to my knowledge, every historian championing Lafayette has somehow managed to skip over this sentence. Even if it be not considered as furnishing reason for suspicion in regard to what he left undone on the 5th of October, it is surely worth quoting because it throws such a flood of light on the political perspicacity of the man.
³ Lafayette uses a very full brush in painting the dangers which he had to brave. He writes: "A diverses reprises le fatal réverbère fut descendu pour lui; vingt fois il fut couché en joue."—Mém. de Lafayette, I. 282.

When Lafayette wrote down his recollections, his memory played him many a trick. Not only is his chronology of the fatal day strangely at fault; he forgets to record that a partisan of his—Vauvilliers, a member of the municipal council—announced to the ministers some hours before it became a fact, that the *whole* national guard had started for Versailles to bring the king to Paris, that he himself sent an adjutant to the municipal council to insist upon his being authorized to march to Versailles, that the council sent four delegates along with him, who were to demand, among other things, that the king " confide the guarding of his sacred person exclusively to the national guard of Paris and Versailles," and transfer his residence to Paris. Irrelevant these facts are certainly not, and scanning them in the light of the position which the 5th of October created for the general, one cannot help asking oneself, whether his silence upon them is quite accidental.[1] One of the most suggestive documents

---

[1] His narrative is comparatively brief, but he finds space to intimate twice that his virtue was even superior to his courage, and that but for the purity of his heart the day might eventually have raised him to the dizziest height. In Paris the spokesman of the former gardes-françaises, who were among the first to raise the cry " à Versailles," apostro-

bearing upon the history of the fatal day is a caricature, representing a white horse with Lafayette's head, led by a proletarian armed with pike and axe; the legend reads: "My friends, lead me, I beg you, to sleep at Versailles."

Though it cannot be directly proved that Lafayette rather liked to be led to Versailles, circumstantial evidence renders it likely. That the Duke of Orleans and those who made the impotent ambition of the dissolute prince a means to serve their own impure ends, had taken a very active part in kindling the fire, is as good as proved.[1]

phized him thus: "Mon général, le roi nous trompe tous et vous comme les autres; il faut le déposer; son enfant sera roi, vous serez régent, et tout ira bien"; and in Versailles, upon entering the royal palace, he repelled with a smart apropos the denunciatory greeting "Cromwell!"

[1] Grace Dalrymple Elliott writes in her *Journal of my Life during the French Revolution* (pp. 37, 38): "The Duke of Orleans was certainly not at Versailles on that dreadful morning (the 6th), for he breakfasted with company at my house when he was accused of being in the queen's apartment disguised... He expressed himself as not approving of the bringing of the king to Paris: 'that it must be a scheme of Lafayette's,' but added, 'I dare say that they will accuse me of it, as they lay every tumult to my account. I think myself this is a mad project, and like all Lafayette does.'" Apart from the absurd accusation as to his being in the queen's apartment, this, of course, proves nothing. Such a breakfast-table was not the place to unbosom himself

That it could have been kept under control by acting promptly and with energy is demonstrated by the fact, that without recourse to powder and lead or steel, the Hôtel de Ville was cleared of the rabble, holding for a while complete possession of it, carrying away the arms, ransacking the drawers for money, and even attempting to set fire to the building.

Meanwhile part of the women had started for Versailles. Threats of fiendish bestiality against the queen [1] and the presence of men disguised as women in the crowd, indicated only too clearly that terrible things had to be expected. Every female encountered on the march, whether young or old, clothed in rags or in elegant attire, was forced to join the procession. Arrived at Versailles the horde first paid its respects to the National Assembly. The wenches made themselves com-

without reserve. It is, however, not improbable that he said what he thought. But did he say all he thought? He could, indeed, not be benefited by having the king brought to Paris. He rests under the accusation, that according to his programme the 5th of October should be the last day of the reign, perhaps even of the life of Louis XVI., and the 6th the first day of his own regency. That the man, who afterwards cast a formal vote for the death of the head of his family, was none too good to pursue such a scheme, is certain.

[1] Taine, I. 133.

fortable in the seats of the representatives and bade them "shut up," as they had not come to listen to long-winded speeches, but to get bread. But when Mirabeau hurled a sharp rebuke into their faces, they lustily applauded him. The president [1] was made to lead a deputation of the shrews to the king. On foot he trudged through rain and mud at the head of them to the palace, surrounded by the boisterous crowd, jesting and threatening, laughing and cursing. In the hall of the Assembly, a duchess of the street seated herself in his chair.

When at last, late in the evening, Lafayette arrived with the national guard, he assured the king that he had nothing more to fear. Louis submitted to whatever he was asked to do; only in regard to the transfer of his residence did he give an evasive answer.

Upon an examination of the question, whether Lafayette did all he could and ought to have done to make good his promise that the public peace and order would be no more disturbed, I can, to my regret, not enter. I can only mention that the account of La Marck, who speaks as an eye- and-ear-witness, throws a strange light upon the

[1] Mounier.

general's own story. Whether he be blamable or not, the promise was not fulfilled. Early in the morning the mob penetrated into the palace by an unguarded side-entrance. Over the corpses of those who tried to bar their way they rushed to the apartments of the queen. Marie Antoinette had barely time to save herself into the rooms of the king. In the letter to D'Estaing, which I mentioned before, Louis had written: "The Frenchman is incapable of a regicide." Lafayette arrived in time to prevent this assertion being put to a severer test. When Louis stepped out on a balcony and announced his willingness to go to Paris, he was enthusiastically cheered. Against the queen, however, the delirious rabble continued to hurl the fiercest curses and imprecations, until Lafayette led her out on the balcony and kissed her hand. In that moment, he says, the peace was concluded. Yes, the peace which, by way of the guillotine, led to the graveyard.

A few hours later the royal family was on its way to Paris, and the National Assembly resolved never to separate itself from the king. Royalty had formally struck its flag before the mob and accepted the rabble as its master. But that was by far not all. The mob had trampled into the dust every one of the constituted authorities. It is for this reason that the 5th and 6th of October are the most portentous, the darkest days of the revolution. The municipal council and the commander-in-chief of the national guard had, according to their own confession, received the law from the mob, and the National Assembly had not merely been unable to stem the torrent; like the municipal council and the national guard it had been treated to contemptuous kicks, and like them it had submitted to being pressed into the service of the mob. On the 5th and 6th of October the proletariat of the capital made itself the *de facto* sovereign of France. This fact is the main key to the whole subsequent history of the revolution. This time the proletariat had become completely conscious of the full scope and purport of its victory. Would it ever again scruple or hesitate to dictate the law to the city government, the *bourgeoisie* in uniform, the king, the National Assembly, when it saw fit to do so? Would it ever again doubt its ability to do it, after having succeeded so completely? Henceforth a wearisome march of many miles was no longer required. Week in and week out, day and night, were its fingers around the throat of the king and the

National Assembly, and therewith around the throat of France.

What, on the 30th of August, Mirabeau had declared " a thousand times more disastrous than the dissolution of the Assembly by a stroke of despotism," had, in a modified form, come to pass. Did he still think as he had thought then?

Quite a while before the vanguard of the women arrived at Versailles he notified the President of the Assembly that, as he expressed himself, "Paris marches upon us," urging him to hasten to the palace in order to have the necessary measures taken for parrying the impending blow. Mounier, who deeply distrusted the impetuous tribune, refused to give credence to the information. When Mirabeau vouched for its truth and with an air of peremptoriness insisted upon his advice, Mounier replied: "Paris marches upon us; well! so much the better, we shall all the sooner be a republic."[1]

On the 10th of October, Malouet demanded proscriptive declarations against libellous writings exciting the people to acts of violence. Mirabeau rose in opposition, saying: "Do not multiply vain declarations; revive the executive power; know

[1] Buchez et Roux, III. 78.

how to maintain it; brace it by all the support that can be derived from the good citizens; else society falls into dissolution and nothing can save us from the horrors of anarchy."[1]

On the 14th he introduced a rigorous bill against *attroupements*, an imitation, as he himself said, of the English *Riot Act*.[2]

Was it not a pretty bold undertaking in the face of these public utterances and acts to suspect his position towards the events of the 5th and 6th? Ought they not to have been convincing to every unprejudiced mind? But let us suppose that other facts or alleged facts, upon which I cannot enter, left ample room for reasonable doubts. Time, upon which he often declared he must rely for his vindication, has brought a document to light which answers the question in such a way, that, as to it, malice itself can no longer discover the shadow of a rent in his armor.

If there was a man in France, whom the storm bursting forth on the 5th did not take by surprise, it was he. Towards the end of September, as La Marck tells us, he often said, speaking of the court: "What are these people thinking of? Do they not see the abysses opening up under their

[1] Œuvres, II. 271.   [2] Ib., II. 278, *sq.*

fect?" One day he exclaimed: "All is lost; the king and the queen will perish, and you will see it; the populace will kick their corpses." La Marck looking at him aghast with horror, he emphatically repeated: "Yes, yes, they will kick their corpses; you do not sufficiently understand the dangers of their position; but their eyes ought to be opened to them."[1]

Now, on the 7th of October, Mirabeau went to La Marck and told him: "If you have any means to make yourself heard by the king and the queen, convince them that France and they are lost if the royal family do not leave Paris. I am working at a plan to get them out of it; will you be able to go to them and assure them that they can count upon me?"[2] La Marck promised to deliver the plan, and a few days later Mirabeau gave him the remarkable document which is known as the Memoir of the 15th of October.[3] The *bailli* had once said of him: "His head is a mill of thoughts and ideas." Perhaps at no other moment of his life did he justify this word more than then. With truly miraculous celerity he ties the warp of an astounding, all-embracing plan,

[1] Corresp., I. 112. [2] Ib., I. 119.
[3] Ib., I. 364–382.

and everything indicates that, if his arm is but left free, he will be able to weave in the woof with equal celerity.

The Memoir begins by stating that neither the king nor the National Assembly is free in Paris, *i. e.*, Mirabeau starts from the point which was in fact absolutely decisive for the whole subsequent course of the revolution. Then he proceeds to ask, whether the king is at least personally quite safe, and answers this question thus: "In the situation in which he is, the slightest catastrophes could compromise this safety. . . The excited mob of Paris is irresistible; winter approaches, provisions may be scarce, bankruptcy may ensue. What will Paris be three months hence? Certainly a hospital, perhaps a theatre of horrors." The ministers, he continues, are without any resources. Only Necker, whom he calls "a truly empty head," still enjoys some popularity, but he does not know how to use it. Then he goes on: "The provinces are not as yet torn asunder, but they observe each other; a covert dissension announces storms. The exchange of provisions is more and more interrupted. The number of malcontents increases by the inevitable effect of the justest decrees of the National Assembly. A nation is in essence nothing but what its labor is. The nation has become disused to work. The public force lies in public opinion and the revenues of the state; all the ties of public opinion are severed and only the direct taxes are paid and even these but in part, while half of our taxes are indirect ones. It will require several years to restore what six months have destroyed, and the impatience of the people, stimulated by distress, manifests itself on all sides."

Besides, circumstances steadily press on towards another disastrous event. The National Assembly, organized upon a wrong principle and composed of too heterogeneous elements, loses every day more and more the public confidence. "It is pushed beyond its own principles by the pernicious irrevocability with which it has invested its first decrees, and, not daring either to contradict itself or to retrace its steps, it has made its very power another obstacle. . . . A dull commotion is setting in, which can in one day destroy the fruits of the greatest exertions; the body politic falls into dissolution; a crisis is necessary to regenerate it; it needs a transfusion of fresh blood.

"The only means to save the state and the

nascent constitution is to bring the king into a situation which will allow him to unite himself instantly with his people.

"For a long time Paris has swallowed up all the revenues of the state. Paris is the seat of the fiscal régime abhorred by the provinces; Paris has created the public debt; Paris has ruined the public credit and compromised the honor of the nation by its pernicious stock-jobbing. Shall now the National Assembly also see nothing but this one city and for its sake plunge the whole kingdom into perdition? . . . What is one to do? Is the king free? His freedom is not complete; it is not recognized.

"Is the king safe? I do not think so. Can Paris save itself? No; Paris is lost, if it be not brought back to order, if it be not forced into moderation."

Then he proceeds to discuss the question, how one can extricate oneself from the appalling situation, and by what means the impending dangers can be averted.

"Several means are available, but among them are some which would unfetter the direst evils, and I mention them only to divert the king from them as his inevitable ruin.

"To withdraw to Metz, or any other point on the frontier, would be to declare war to the nation and abdicate. A king, who is the only protection of his people, does not fly from his people; he lets it be the judge of his acts and principles, but does not sever at one blow all the bonds uniting him with it; he does not arouse against himself the universal distrust; he does not put himself into such a situation that he can return to his state only with arms in his hands, or is reduced to beg the aid of foreign countries.

"And who can calculate how far the exaltation of the French nation would go, if it were to see itself abandoned by its king to unite himself with the proscribed and become himself one; how far it might go in arming itself for resistance and defying the forces he could muster against it? After such an event I should myself denounce the king.

"To retire into the interior of the kingdom and to summon the whole nobility would not be less dangerous. Whether it be justified or not, the whole nation, in its ignorance confounding the nobility with the patriciate, will, for a long time, consider the noblemen, as a class, their most implacable enemies. The abolition of the feudal system was an atonement due to ten centuries of madness. One could have moderated the movement, but now it is too late, and the sentence is irrevocable. To unite himself with the nobility would be worse than to throw himself into the arms of a foreign and hostile army; that would be to choose between a great nation and some individuals, between peace and civil war with extremely unequal forces.

"Where would be in such a case the safety of the king? A corps of noblemen is not an army which could wage war; a province cannot entrench itself. Would not the greatest part of this nobility be crushed, killed, even before uniting? Would its estates not be destroyed? And if it were only summoned to bring the greatest sacrifices, the mortal blow would be dealt ere one could exchange views and come to an understanding; and if one intended to preserve to the nobility all of its exemptions and privileges that public opinion and enlightened reason have destroyed, does one believe that peace, that the revenues could be restored in a nation, which thereby would be robbed of its dearest and most justified hopes?

"To go away in order to regain liberty, denounce the National Assembly and dissolve every connection with it, would be a less violent course than the two preceding ones, but not less dangerous; it would endanger the safety of the king; it would also inaugurate civil war, because many of the provinces want to maintain the decrees of the Assembly . . . because the enlightened part of this nation knows that one must provisionally obey even the errors of a legislative body, without which no constitution whatever could ever be established. Then neither the nobility, whose passions he does not share, nor the nation, whose intents he does not accept, would be for the king. . . .

"Besides it is certain that a great revolution is needed to save the kingdom, that the nation has rights, that it is about to regain them all, that they must not only be restored, but also consolidated, that only a national convention can regenerate France, that the National Assembly has made several laws which it is indispensable to accept, and that there is no safety for the king and the state but in the closest coalition between the monarch and the people."

Only one means is left, "which is certainly not without danger; but one must not believe that one can get out of a great danger without danger, and all the forces of the statesmen must now be exerted to prepare, to moderate, to direct, and to limit the crisis, but not to prevent it, for that is absolutely impossible, nor to postpone it, for that would only serve to make it more violent.

"This last plan can be carried out by simple means. Of course these means should be prepared beforehand down almost to the minutest details. Only at the moment the resolution is taken should they be communicated to those who are to employ them. The cabinet is not sufficiently well-meaning, or at least not considered to be so, to admit it into the confidence. It is a last resource of the public weal and the personal welfare of the king. All would be lost, if indiscretions were to reveal a plan which might be considered a conspiracy, if its aim and consequences be not known, while its only object is the welfare of the state."

Then follows the sketch of the plan.

While the arrangements for the departure of the king are being made, public opinion in the provinces must be prepared for the impending events. The progress of events will unquestionably demonstrate with ever increasing impressiveness the fact that the king is not free. The national guard of Paris is sure to step out of its legitimate functions, if one tries to confine it to them. By asking the support of the National Assembly, its eyes will be opened to its own situation and it will see its own existence imperilled. Thus it will become more and more patent that the public welfare imperatively demands the departure of the king. To insure the departure, his guards shall be "systematically dispersed," and under different pretexts an army of 10,000 men organized, consisting entirely of national regiments to be placed midway between Paris and Rouen. Then the king shall depart for Rouen in broad daylight. Rouen shall be chosen, first, because it is in the interior of the kingdom, thereby precluding the suspicion that the king intends to fly, then, because from there Paris can be provisioned and thus the good intentions of the king be demonstrated, and finally, because the Normandie has a numerous and energetic population, and Bretagne and Anjou, being also loyal, are within easy reach. Simultaneously with the departure a proclamation shall be issued, declaring that the king throws himself into the arms of his people, because violence had been done to him at Versailles; that he, as he would prove, had been denied the right of every citizen to come and go as he pleased; that this situation had served as a pretext to the malcontents to refuse obedience to the decrees of the National Assembly, thereby compromising the fruits of a revolution, in which he took as lively an interest as the most zealous friends of liberty; that he wished to be inseparable from his people, as he had irrefutably proved by choosing Rouen as the place of his residence; that he was the first king of France wishing to give the nation its rights, and that he had persisted in his intentions, despite his ministers and other advices calculated to corrupt monarchs; that he had irrevocably sanctioned such and such decrees of the National Assembly, but that there were others, which he deemed not sufficiently considered or advantageous enough for the people, and that he therefore desired the people to examine them once more, acknowledging, however, their binding force as laws in the meantime; that he would ask the National Assembly to join him in order to continue its labors, but would soon call another convention to examine, confirm, modify, and ratify the decrees of the first; that he wished, above all, the public debt to be considered sacred; that he was willing personally to submit to the greatest sacrifices and would not require more than one million a year; that the public creditors should no longer be allured by vain promises, but receive an adequate security; that he would subdue his people not by arms, but by his love, confiding his honor and safety to French loyalty; that he wished only the welfare of the citizens and wanted to be only a citizen himself.—Couriers should bring this very firm, but very popular proclamation into all the provinces.—Another proclamation should be sent to the National Assembly, setting forth the motives for the king's resolution and asking it to follow him to Rouen. It would undoubtedly do so, if it were free; if it could not do it, the session would thereby *ipso facto* be closed. The Assembly's being under constraint would become so apparent that it would soon be possible to convene another Assembly. Further proclamations should continue to enlighten the people about their true interests, and the changing of public opinion would soon commence to work a change in the spirit of the National Assembly. If anywhere resistance should be attempted, the executive, authorized by the National Assembly, would use its whole power to overcome it.

Nothing came of the plan. La Marck gave the Memoir to the Count of Provence, the king's eldest brother. He praised Mirabeau's intentions, but treated it as an interesting academical treatise, declaring—no doubt only too truly—that it was impossible to induce the king to take so bold a course. But though the Memoir led to no practical results, it is one of the most remarkable political documents in existence. Its critical part shows the whole subsequent history of the revolution as in a magician's mirror, and this whole subsequent history of the revolution irrefutably proves, that if there still was any possibility to save the king's head and spare France the reign of terror and the ensuing despotism of Napoleon, it could have been done only by adopting Mirabeau's plan and entrusting its execution to him. If the records of everything else we know of Mirabeau were forever obliterated, this one Memoir would suffice to prove that he was a political genius of the very first order. Only the utter imbecility of fanatical doctrinarianism can find in it materials for the charge that he became a recreant and turned against the revolution, whose foremost champion he had thus far been. Every line of it demonstrates that, in fact, his whole mind was bent upon not only maintaining, but also, as he said, consolidating the revolution in saving it despite itself from itself. There was no other way to do this than by appealing from Paris to the country, and to do it now and in such a manner, that the country could respond to the appeal not only by sentiments and wishes, but by decisive acts. And this was possible only if the king accompanied the appeal by the explicit and emphatic declaration of his identification with the revolution, guaranteeing the unimpeachable sincerity of the declaration by irreversible acts.

It is not surprising that, at the time, many strongly suspected or even firmly believed Mirabeau to be one of the principal authors of the 5th of October. In their opinion the sins of his youth were sufficient evidence that moral scruples would never be a check to his political ambition; his political past, of which they noticed or understood only the one side, that of the revolutionary firebrand, seemed to them in perfect keeping with a manœuvre of such brazen ruthlessness; and many an inconsiderate *à propos* of his rash and unruly tongue furnished strong pegs to distrust and jealousy, hatred and stupidity, on which to hang plausible accusations. These people were so blindfolded by prejudice, that they simply ignored the incompatibility of their assumptions with the public utterances and acts of Mirabeau which I mentioned. When the National Assembly decided that the facts elicited by the judicial inquiry conducted by the Chatelet gave no cause to proceed against him, they remained satisfied that it was a miscarriage of justice. They grievously wronged him; but in these times, when morbid suspiciousness became more and more one of the cardinal virtues, their error was, under the circumstances, almost excusable. But what shall one say of the writers of to-day who, with the Memoir of the 15th before their eyes, still persist in putting every particle of those incriminating baubles under the microscope of their critical acumen, and at least intimate that there is no telling whether he was not, after all, for a while and to some extent, in collusion with the conspirators? La Marck relates that when he told Mirabeau half a year later that, up to that time, even the queen had supposed the charge to be well-founded, "his mien instantly changed; he became yellow, green, hideous. The horror which he felt was striking ... for a long time he could not get over the painful impression that he should have been the object of such a horrid suspicion."[1] Small wonder! The man who said that the course he urged upon the king would be considered " a conspiracy," and who had predicted before the October events that the mob would " kick the corpses of the king and the queen," could not have failed to see that by the Memoir of the 15th he put his own head under the executioner's axe. To say that he had had a share in the conspiracy is, therefore, to say that he had helped to hatch and execute a criminal plot, possibly leading to regicide and sure to cost human life, for the purpose of attempting, right after its complete success, to undo at the risk of his own neck what he had done. The assumption is a palpable absurdity. Since the publication of the Memoir of the 15th, Mirabeau's accusers have, therefore, no longer any standing in the court of common sense. It takes learned historians to still grant them a hearing and gravely to wag their wise heads at the awful things they have to report of the great miscreant.

[1] Corresp., I, 148, 149.

LECTURE IX.

The Decisive Defeat of November 7th, 1789.

NOT intellect and character, but character and intellect are required to be a leader of men, and the more so the stormier the times and the greater the issues. Mirabeau invariably rested his claims to leadership primarily upon his character and not upon his superior intellect. One of the chief tests of character, however, is the effect of obstacles and defeats upon the will. With weak men it always slackens under their pressure, though they be intellectually veritable paragons; upon the strong character it has a bracing effect, and acts as a spur.

If Mirabeau had misjudged himself as to this paramount question, the shelving of the Memoir of the 15th of October by the Count de Provence as an interesting academical treatise would have been a staggering blow, for it proved that from those who were personally the most interested in it, no assistance could be expected in intelligent efforts to avert the impending doom of the monarchy; it had to be saved without them and in spite of them, or it could not be saved at all. It is therefore eminently characteristic of the man, that at no time is his initiative more vigorous and buoyant than in the weeks immediately following this grievous disappointment.

On the 14th of October he had submitted to the Assembly a law concerning "*les attroupements,*" "imitating," as he said, "but not copying" the English Riot Act. When he had finished reading it, the Assembly vividly applauded but did not act upon it until, a week later, the mob in Paris had once more dipped its hands in blood, massacring the baker François upon the accusation that he reserved some of his bread for customers able and willing to pay higher prices. Mirabeau then improved the opportunity to warn the Assembly that though a martial law was necessary, the most urgent need was to put the executive again into a condition enabling it to fulfil its duties. "The executive power avails itself of its own annihilation," he said.[1] And to guard against an unjust, one-sided interpretation of this accusation, he wrote in the *Courrier de Provence* : "Not without reason

[1] Œuvres, II. 294.

does the cabinet avail itself of its own annihilation to hold itself excused in regard to the disorders of society; if it has no power (*s'il ne peut rien*), it is not responsible for anything." [1]

Still nothing was further from his mind than the intention fully to exonerate the ministers. In his opinion they were—not intentionally, but by incapacity—highly culpable, but the Assembly was at least as guilty as they. He wrote in these days to Mauvillon: " The monarchy is in danger rather because one does not govern, than because one conspires. If no pilot presents himself, the vessel will probably run aground. If, on the contrary, the force of things compels to call a man of brains, and furnishes the courage to conquer all human deferences and the petty jealousy which will always try to prevent it, you do not imagine how easy it is to make the public vessel float. The resources of this country, even the mobility of this nation, which is its cardinal vice, furnish so many expedients and facilities, that in France one must never either presume or despair." [2] He is satisfied that the future depends on having the right men at the helm more than on anything else; but he sees as clearly, that in this tempestuous and

[1] No. 56.   [2] Lettres à Mauvillon, 488.

reef-bound sea, the ship must be sailing toward destruction even with the best men at the helm, if they be denied the possibility of making use of their strength and their skill. Neither by striking the shackles off the arms of the present utterly incapable ministers, nor by putting efficient but equally fettered men in their chairs, could the perils of the situation successfully be coped with. Only if a proper change of persons and a proper change of system in regard to the position of the executive and its relation towards the legislative could be brought about simultaneously, would the hope that the revolution might be turned back and kept down to its legitimate task of reform, rest upon a more solid foundation than mere wishes.

That Mirabeau did not need the lesson of the 5th and 6th of October fully to understand this, is proved by the fact, that three weeks before, an article of the *Courrier de Provence* (Sept. 14) had already advocated the remedy which he proposed in the Assembly on the 6th of November. On the 9th and 15th of October the *Courrier* had returned to the charge. The articles may not have been written by himself, but the paper was his organ, and nobody could suppose it to act without his authorization in a question of such moment.

Above all, however, he had as early as September 29th, and in the Assembly itself, explicitly declared in favor of following the example of England, and demanded that the question be taken up and decided.[1] The charge which Montlosier preferred against him on the 7th of November, that he had sprung a mine upon the Assembly by his motion, was therefore wholly unfounded.

It cannot, however, be doubted, that but for those two October days Mirabeau would have proceeded more slowly. They forced upon him the conviction that not a day might be lost with impunity. From that moment all his energies are bent upon carrying out the double programme. Without Lafayette's consent and co-operation this was unquestionably an impossible task. For weeks he and his friends, supported ostensibly with ardor by Cicé, the Archbishop of Bordeaux and keeper of the seals, are day and night at work to bring about an alliance with the general. For this purpose the two men met on the 15th or 16th of October at Passy, in the house of the Marquise d'Aragon, Mirabeau's niece. This first conversation was mutually deemed sufficiently satisfactory to continue the negotiations. Our material con-

[1] Moniteur, No. 65, pp. 532, 533.

cerning them is unfortunately neither ample nor definite enough to get a perfectly clear idea of them. Too much must be read between the lines and even guessed. The difficulties are trebled by the fact that for a while a purely personal question, Mirabeau's pecuniary embarrassments, is in such a way mixed up with the great political question, that it is impossible to separate the two; they are, so to speak, intergrown. Lafayette was to procure him, directly or indirectly, by the appointment to an ambassadorship, the pecuniary aid he stood in need of, and this was in a way to form the basis of the pact. Mirabeau's wants were so urgent that he might have succumbed, or, at least, come desperately near succumbing to the temptation of buying relief at the expense of his ambition and patriotism, if his rich and open-handed friend La Marck had not repeatedly assured him that he would never allow him to sink under the load of his debts. Mirabeau soon became all the more willing to rely upon these promises as Lafayette sent him not quite half the amount he had undertaken to get for him. The money was promptly returned, and every idea of going for the sake of the money with a big title into virtual exile, definitely abandoned. But that was not all.

On the 26th of October he informs La Marck that Montmorin has proposed to Lafayette to nominate him, Mirabeau, ambassador to Holland or England, "not to go there, but to decorate me and to render me worthy and fit for the supreme honor of having in my pocket a promise from the king which assures me that I shall be minister next May." "Lafayette," concludes the important letter, "is to speak only this morning to the queen, but, to tell the truth, he seemed to me less decided than ever, and succumbing under the fatality of his indecision. As to myself, I shall resume the combat, firmly resolved —*what is in their own interest if it be true that they think me necessary*—not to lose an inch of ground, and convinced that at the very latest by the end of next month, everything will go to smash."[1] La Marck replied: "This would be acceptable, if all this were not, as you have strong reasons to anticipate, to go to smash before the end of next month."

La Marck was not as much given to using strong language as Mirabeau, and at this time he still took a much less gloomy view of the future. His ready assent to Mirabeau's prophecy, therefore,

[1] Corresp., I. 406, 407.

leaves no doubt that, as is to be inferred from the whole situation and the general tenor of the correspondence of the two friends at this period, their lugubrious prediction is not intended to be as sweeping as at first sight the "everything" would seem to indicate. They only refer to the cabinet and what is directly in connection with and dependent on this question. In their opinion the present administration can no longer be saved, neither by the passive resistance of the king, nor by all the small devices of the ministers themselves, clinging most tenaciously to their chairs, though their seats are cushions of thorns. And Mirabeau is determined himself to do his best for the fulfilment of his prophecy.

You remember that from the beginning he had charged the ministers with matchless ineptitude. It therefore goes without saying that, if he could have acted entirely to suit himself, he would also now from the first have declined to listen to any other proposition, peremptorily insisting upon their being compelled to go. But to gain at once Lafayette's consent to such a radical course was utterly out of the question. He considered it, above all, almost a sacrilege to think of overthrowing Necker. Mirabeau, as we know, deemed him the worst of all, and the general certainly did not put his own political acumen into the best light by still having so much faith in the financial necromancer, whose only miracles, ever since the convocation of the States-General, consisted in the rapidity and thoroughness with which he destroyed his reputation as a great financier and statesman. But this did not alter the fact that Lafayette's support was indispensable. Mirabeau, therefore, so far yielded as to enter upon negotiations with the ministers, but he did it reluctantly and without abandoning even for the moment the intention to bring all the pressure within his power to bear upon Lafayette, to frighten him into adopting his views. On the 17th of October he informs La Marck, that in the forenoon the general is to bring him to Montmorin, and that in the afternoon he is to see Necker, who is mad about it and has only consented because he is at bay and feels the knife to be at his throat. Then the letter continues: "Lafayette, who is alarmed by the question of provisioning (Paris) and uneasy about the provinces, must be forced to come to a decision. I myself am resolved to support the motion of Necker's resignation (*départ*), so deeply am I convinced that everything is perishing." [1]

The interview with Necker lasted five hours. According to Mme. de Staël, Necker said in the course of it: "My strength consists in morality; you have too much *esprit* not to feel some day the necessity of this support; until that moment has come, it may suit the king under the actual circumstances to have you for minister, but we two cannot be ministers at the same time." Mirabeau did not fail to acknowledge and reciprocate the compliment. On the 19th he wrote Lafayette: "If you have reflected upon the perfidious collusion of the ministers with the brutal or rather truly delirious pride of the despicable charlatan (Necker) who has brought the throne and France within an inch of their ruin, and who persists in rather consummating it than to acknowledge to himself his incapacity, you do not believe any more that I can be in the least their auxiliary.

"They have insulted me, marked me out; they have tried, so far as they could, to denounce my ambition and the difficulties which I throw in their way; they could only disarm me in oper-

[1] Corresp., I. 385.

ating the public welfare, and the evil spirit of the human race is not further from that than they. Permit me to entreat you, that you no longer demand from me that I spare them and that . . . I may at last enable the nation to judge, whether the actual cabinet can save the state."[1] He tells him, that the very next day he will attack the ministers, and he is as good as his word.

Two days later La Marck warned him not to precipitate matters; just because his becoming minister was an imperative necessity, he should not risk anything. Mirabeau did not spurn the advice. The negotiations went on, but, as I mentioned, came to naught, and Lafayette could not make up his mind what to do. Three days after Mirabeau had informed La Marck of Montmorin's offer and his determination to reject it, Lafayette writes him, underlining the sentence: "What would you say, if Necker should threaten to go in case Mirabeau arrives," *i. e.*, is made minister? It is hard to tell what to make of this question. Is it to him still so much a matter of course, that Necker's going would be the greatest calamity, that he, in spite of everything, assumes even Mirabeau will shrink back if he learns that

[1] Corresp., I. 389, 390.

this would be the consequence of his entering the cabinet? This would seem to be the most natural interpretation, if Talon had not reported the same day to La Marck, that he had found the general dissatisfied with Necker, "positively announcing that the wheel will turn to-day."

For two or three days the go-betweens seem to have been very confident of complete success. It is likely that two undated lists of ministers in Mirabeau's handwriting were projected in these days. One of them is headed by Necker's name as prime-minister, but with the remark: "Because one must render him as powerless as he is incapable, and at the same time preserve his popularity to the king." Mirabeau figures in it as member of the cabinet, but without any special department. To his name the remark is added: "The petty scruples of human deference are no more in season. The government must loudly announce that its foremost auxiliaries will be henceforth sound principles, character, and talent." Lafayette is to be a member of the cabinet with the title of "*Maréchal de France*," and temporarily invested with the office of commander-in-chief for the purpose of reorganizing the army.— The second list is incomplete and divided into two groups, respectively headed: "Part of Lafayette," and "Part of the Queen." [1]

One is evidently on the eve of the decision, but, unfortunately, the more we approach it, the more fragmentary also our sources become. Thus much we can see, that both sides are equally active in getting ready for the battle. Lafayette has, after all, again failed to "turn the wheel." His exasperating consistency in swinging like a pendulum from right to left and back from left to right nothing can overcome. Talon writes, on the 5th of November, to La Marck: "I am going to Lafayette; we shall do the impossible to determine him." And in the same note he says: "A terrible plot, I repeat it, is being formed against Mirabeau in the Assembly." [2] This is no news to Mirabeau. He writes on the same day to La Marck: "The bomb of my enemies is to explode on Monday" (the 9th). And he knows as well that the ministers do not propose to be led like sheep to the slaughter-house. On the 6th he informs La Marck, that they have had a conference at Lafayette's, who, he declares, was mad about them on the 4th, but is completely duped by them. But he is in high spirits. He is determined to

[1] Corresp., I. 411, 412.   [2] Ib., I. 416.

head them off. On the 5th he announces to **La Marck**, that he will attack them the next day and tells him how he intends to do it. I do not see, he says, what miracle could make these gentlemen live, if from Monday next they can get no dollar more, and "are to-morrow compelled to accept or refuse the honor of seating themselves among us." A victory, which he achieved on that day in another question over the cabinet, elates him so much that he writes on the morning of the 6th to La Marck, that his cause has advanced "at giant strides." Lafayette, he thinks, will be compelled to surrender practically at discretion, grateful that his (Mirabeau's) " personal fidelity " will cede to him the honor of presenting the list of ministers, which he (Mirabeau) will compose for him.

The letter states that he proposes to open the attack "by a simple tactical evolution." M. Loménie infers from this expression that the financial question, which was the order of the day, only served him as a "pretext." If tnis be correct, his further strictures upon the speech cannot be refuted. He charges the remarks upon the financial problems with being "somewhat lengthy," and asserts that Mirabeau, after having entertained the

Assembly "for an hour with these preliminaries, came abruptly, and almost without transition, to the true object of his discourse." If so, then at least on this occasion Mirabeau evidently cuts a rather sorry figure as an orator. That is all the more surprising, because he had had ample time for preparation and intended to strike a decisive blow. M. Loménie ought to have been struck by this as much as the most ardent admirer of Mirabeau, for the one thing in which he acknowledges him to have been a master mind is oratory. He, therefore, must hold others excused if with them the suspicion is aroused that the fault may lie not with Mirabeau, but with him. In my opinion it is one of Mirabeau's greatest speeches, but M. Loménie could not do him justice as an orator, because perhaps in no other case has he so strikingly proved his inability fully to understand and appreciate him as a statesman. Mirabeau does not seize upon the financial question as a pretext, does not waste an hour in irrelevant preliminaries, is not driven to take abruptly an awkward side-leap in order to get at last somehow to his true object. The financial question had been the immediate occasion for convening the States-General; the financial question had continued to be one of the main propelling forces of the revolution; the financial question became every week more the most pressing and the most immediately dangerous problem, the financial question had broadened into the question of the whole economical condition of the country, disintegrating more and more not only the political, but the whole social structure—so long as no efficacious remedy was applied to the financial distress and the rapidly progressing vitiation of the whole economical condition of the country, every day was in itself a "giant-stride" further towards the abyss, and, finally, no remedy could be efficacious, unless the axe was laid to the main root of the evils, that threatened to let the revolution terminate in chaos. Therefore, whatever the order of the day, he had to make the financial question the basis of his argument, if he wanted to treat the problem confronting France *ex fundamento* and argue as a statesman. On this basis he builds with a master's hand. There are no prolixities, no irrelevancies, no sophistries, no captivating oratorical flourishes. It is a matter-of-fact speech, closely knit and of flawless logic: not an argument manufactured for the purpose of arriving at a predetermined conclusion, but an array of irrefutable facts constituting an unbreakable chain leading straight up to the conclusion. But from beginning to end it is the reasoning not of the political metaphysician operating with the logical categories of the school, but of the statesman fully conscious that he must shape his course according to the merciless logic of facts and therefore never lose sight of the whole, viewing and judging everything in its relation to and its bearing upon the whole. This M. Loménie fails to do. The point of view from which he judges speech and speaker is not the whole situation, but the isolated fact that Mirabeau wants to overthrow the cabinet and become minister himself. Choosing this point of view he does not look to the speech for the correct interpretation of the announcement that the attack will be opened by a simple tactical evolution, but this announcement is, without any proof, assumed to furnish the key to the speech, *i. e.*, to be a formal avowal that he will not attempt to conquer by proving, but intends to outmanœuvre the adversary by stratagems. In fact the tactical evolution consisted only in keeping as much as possible all personal questions out of view. Not by attacking the ministers did he propose to get rid of them, but by putting the cabinet into such a position, that henceforth only able ministers would have any chance of maintaining themselves. Indeed a dexterous tactical move, but also something more than that: the only means to save the country.

Literally not a minute does Mirabeau waste in preliminaries. In the very first sentence he succinctly states the thesis he proposes to prove: among the multiplying financial disorders "are some, the aggravation of which could render all our labors useless;"[1] in other words: if a financial sanitation be not effected, everything is at stake. At the head of the financial disorders he puts the disappearing of specie. "A nation accustomed to the use of specie . . . cannot be deprived of it for any length of time without trouble arising in all its transactions, without the efforts of individuals to sustain them becoming more and more ruinous and preparing very great calamities. These calamities approach at long strides. We are on the eve of a formidable crisis." Commerce can no more procure the specie it needs; everybody hoards it for his own safety; the causes, which drive it out of the country, become every day more active, and yet it is indispensable for the provision trade, on which the maintenance of public

[1] Œuvres, II. 395.

tranquillity so largely depends. "Absolutely nothing is done to combat the calamity of our foreign exchange;" drafts on Paris are so discredited, that they can no longer be negotiated in any commercial place. The *caisse d'escompte* continues to flood the country with its paper money, which is justly looked upon with growing distrust, since the government has begun to dispense it from the obligation to pay on presentation specie for its notes. Necker's very reputation has struck a blow against the public credit. Everybody reasons thus: if ever he is reduced to the necessity of having recourse to such means, all resources must be exhausted. Confidence has vanished and is vanishing more every day. The withdrawal of other securities to the amount of about 200 millions has increased the stringency. All the great commercial centres, and, above all, the capital, are already "reduced to the last expedients." "Are the anxieties of Paris in regard to the supply of provisions not as much the effect of the scarcity of specie and the apprehensions it excites, as of the dark plots, so difficult to understand and so impossible to prove, to which one persists in attributing them?" If an economical catastrophe befall Paris, in consequence of a great number of suspensions, ruin must spread from this centre all over the country. " Would it not be a miracle, upon which no one dare put his trust, if in so general a calamity the social bond did not break; if in default of physical force moral force were to preserve it?

" You undoubtedly ask yourselves, gentlemen, to what these observations are to lead us? To turn us more than ever away from the resource of palliatives, to dread vague hopes, not to expect the return of a happier time except by multiplying our efforts and measures to bring it about, not to go on trying by used-up resources to throw our embarrassments upon those who will come after us. Our efforts would be useless; the reign of delusions is past; experience has taught us too much the perfidy of all means leaving to imagination alone to create the motives of confidence."

If this be beating around the bush with irrelevancies used as pretexts, I am yet to read the first political speech that takes the bull by the horns and states with all the plainness and succinctness that language is capable of, what the speaker is driving at. One only must not, in the face of his express declarations, impute to him that he merely wanted to overthrow the cabinet.

This was not the end, but a means to the end, and but one among several. What he wants is to put an end, once for all, to the policy of palliatives and initiate a radical cure, and he declares and proves that in the nature of things, everything can be but a palliative, unless confidence be restored. "In one word," he says, "one must do away with all the causes destructive of confidence, and put in their place the means, the efficacy of which is discernible to the least trained eyes and sustains itself by the solidity and wisdom of their own construction." Mind: *all* the causes destructive of confidence.

Then he proceeds to state and discuss the means, which, in his opinion, ought to be put in their place. He begins with the supply of provisions, *i. e.*, with the question which more than any one other thing renders Paris a volcano threatening every day a new eruption. He thinks an attempt ought to be made to induce the United States to pay their war-loans by sending France grain.

Next he suggests for the administration of the public debt the establishment of a *caisse nationale* with revenues of its own, commensurate to the obligations to be discharged by it and independent of the ministry of finances. This would not only completely restore the confidence of the creditors of the state by giving them a perfect guarantee that they will always be paid what they have to claim, but also engage this powerful class, in their own interest, in every way to support the *caisse nationale* and the public credit in general.

What more, he then asks, will have to be done, to secure to the nation the credit it deserves? And he answers: "The return of peace and good order, the restoration of the forces of the empire." He pretends to think that one is rapidly advancing on the high-road towards this goal, but declares that it cannot be reached, so long as there is an antagonism between the Assembly and the ministers, and this antagonism, he asserts, must continue, so long as the ministers are absent from the National Assembly. "All good citizens sigh for the re-establishment of the public force; and what public force can we establish if the executive and legislative powers look upon each other as enemies and fear to discuss in common the public affairs?"

That this *was* the pivotal point of the whole political problem, is incontestable. On this occasion Mirabeau assumed it to be so patent, that it required no proof. He at once proceeded to the examination of the question, whether the means, by which he proposed to bring about the necessary concert between the two departments, be adapted to the end.

In England, he said, " the depository of a long course of experiences on liberty," the nation considers the presence of the ministers in Parliament not only absolutely necessary, but one of its great privileges. It thus exercises over all acts of the executive power a control which is more important than any other responsibility.

"There is not a member of the Assembly that cannot interrogate them. The minister cannot help answering ... every question is official, has the whole Assembly as a witness; evasions, equivocations are judged by a great number of men, who have the right to insist upon more explicit answers... What has one to oppose to these advantages? Will it be said that the National Assembly has no need to be informed by the ministers? But where are, in the first place, the facts to be found which constitute the experience of the government?... Can one say that those who execute the laws have nothing to tell to those by whom they are devised and determined? Are the executors of all the public transactions ... not like a repertory, which an active representative of the nation must constantly consult? And where could this be done to greater advantage to the nation than in the presence of the Assembly? Outside the Assembly the inquirer is but an individual, to whom the minister can answer what he likes, and even not answer at all. Will he be interrogated by a decree of the Assembly? But then one exposes oneself to procrastinations, delays, tergiversations, obscure answers... Does one say that the minister can be summoned to appear before the Assembly?... only the majority can summon him, while in the Assembly he cannot escape the interrogatory of a single member.

"Where could the ministers combat with less success the liberty of the people? where will they make with less inconvenience their observations on the acts of legislation? where will their prejudices, their errors, their ambition be unveiled with more energy? where will they contribute more to the stability of the decrees? where will they more solemnly take the obligation to execute them?...

[1] "Does one say that the minister will have more influence in the Assembly than if he had not

---

[1] The paragraph-structure in this and similar quotations may appear a little odd. It is always strictly according to the original.

the right to sit in it? It would be pretty difficult to prove it. The influence of the ministers, if it is not due to their talents and their virtues, springs from manœuvres, seductions, secret corruptions, and if anything can diminish the effect of these, it is when they, as members of the Assembly, are constantly under the eyes of an opposition, which has no interest to spare them.

"Why should we fear the presence of the ministers? Must we dread their vengeance? Is it to be apprehended that they will themselves mark out their victims? One would forget that we are making a free constitution... The laws on individual liberty will liberate us from ministerial despotism. That is the true, the only safeguard of the liberty of votes.

"No, gentlemen, we shall not yield to frivolous fears, to idle phantoms; we will not have that distrustful timidity which rushes into traps from very fear to defy them.

"The first agents of the executive power are necessary in every legislative assembly; they form a part of the organs of its intelligence. The laws, discussed with them, will become more easy; their sanction will be more assured, and their execution more complete. Their presence will prevent incidents, steady our march, promote concert between the two powers to whom the fate of the empire is confided."

He concluded with a threefold motion, covering the three remedies he had suggested. The last one, clad in the form of an invitation to the ministers, conferred upon them " a consultative voice, until definite provision be made in regard to them by the constitution."

So many members vividly applauded the orator that he might well feel confident of success. And even apart from the cogency of his reasoning the Assembly, if it cared anything for being consistent, had indeed good cause for receiving the motion favorably. On the 4th of August the king had notified the Assembly of the appointment of three new ministers.[1] The last sentence of his letter read thus: "By choosing from your Assembly I indicate my desire to entertain with it the most constant and most amiable harmony." Upon demand the letter had to be read a second time and each time it was loudly applauded. Then, state the *Archives Parlementaires*, "upon the

---

[1] The Archbishop of Bordeaux, Champion de Cicé, the Archbishop of Vienne, La France de Pompignan, and de la Tour-du-Pin-Paulin.

motion of several members the Assembly votes
unanimously an address of thanks to the king for
the mark of confidence which he has given it."[1]
The new ministers, it is true, had ceased to occupy
their seats in the Assembly, but, so far as I can see,
not in consequence of any action on the part of
the Assembly; their letter of the 5th of August to
the Assembly is silent on this point.[2] On the
other hand, however, the crown had claimed the
right to send the ministers before the Assembly,
verbally to communicate to it the views of the
government, and the Assembly had not contested
the claim. But three days after that letter of the
king, to which the Assembly unanimously voted to
reply by an address of thanks, the cabinet appeared
before the Assembly, Cicé announcing: "We are
sent to you by the king to deposit in your bosom
the apprehensions agitating the paternal heart of
His Majesty."[3]

Would an opinion, based merely on these facts
and on what was revealed on the surface of the

---

[1] Arch. Parl., IX. 341.

[2] Mirabeau said in the Assembly: "Ils ont jugé à propos
d'abdiquer la titre des réprésentans de la nation ; ils ont cru
bien faire, mais il est permis d'avoir deux avis à cet égard."
—Moniteur, Sept. 29, 1789.

[3] Arch. Parl., IX. 360.

situation, not rather have charged Mirabeau with having set up an unnecessarily huge apparatus for the attainment of his end, than with having undertaken a hopeless task? And the speeches that were made against his motion were eminently calculated to confirm this view. I say speeches, for to say arguments would be an unwarrantable abuse of the word. Blin's speech, the only one with at least a pretence at arguing, was a tissue of gross, self-contradictory sophisms. Instead of refuting Mirabeau, he tears to pieces a man of straw set up by himself. He undertakes to prove the impropriety of consulting with the ministers in the Assembly, by gravely demonstrating that it would not be the proper thing to consult "*only*" the ministers—he pretends to think that the adoption of the motion would preclude the ministers being consulted by committees, because Mirabeau has spoken disparagingly of these—he opposes the motion, now, because the poor ministers ought not to be exposed to the ruthless attacks of ambitious members, and, in the next minute, because they will force all sorts of obnoxious laws upon the Assembly, for their responsibility will have been rendered a " chimerical terror." The experiences of England, according to him, are only the most impressive warning against the motion: if the ministers had not been in Parliament, England would never have lost her American colonies and numberless bad laws would not have been passed. Let the motion be adopted and there is but one alternative: either the executive power is unnecessarily and uselessly depressed and debased, or " the Assembly is no longer free and the nation is in danger of losing its liberty." " The only enemies of the kings and of the nations are the ministers."[1]

This apothegm of political doctrinarianism run mad was the climax of the speech. The climax, but not the true key to it. This was concealed in a vague and enigmatical remark about some " ambition of a near or distant future." Principally to ponder this over-night, and not to digest the argumentative hash to which it had been treated by Blin, the Assembly postponed its decision to the next day. That boded no good. Apparently Mirabeau had every reason to be of good cheer: in fact the battle was virtually lost, for the constitution of the Assembly was such, that it was almost sure to succumb if poison of

[1] Arch. Parl., IX. 711-713.

this kind was allowed to work for twenty-four hours.[1]

The tone which his adversaries assumed the next day, at once apprised Mirabeau that he was defeated. Montlosier excelled Blin in the holy zeal with which he declaimed against allowing the ministers " to enlighten our debates with their false light, to fill them with their false doctrine ; " but his concluding assertion, that the proposition must have " a mystic sense," smartly turned Blin's dagger around in the wound. Lanjuinais, who followed him, disdained to fight with innuendoes. With visor wide-open he struck straight home. "An eloquent genius," he exclaimed, "prevails on you and subjugates you; what would this man not do, if he were to become minister?"[2]

[1] According to the Arch. Parl., Blin spoke on the 6th and 7th. The second speech, however, reads so much like a synopsis of the first that one cannot help suspecting a blunder on the part of the editors, though it is almost too gross to seem credible. If Blin spoke but once, it is as good as certain that he did so on the 7th. In that case the situation would have been apparently still more favorable for Mirabeau, but in fact he had all the more reason to expect a defeat. As his motion had been vigorously supported by some, and none of the other opponents had adduced anything against it bearing even the semblance of a serious argument, the refusal to come to a vote was inexplicable unless it concealed a sinister design.

[2] Œuvres, II. 433. The synopsis of Lanjuinais' speech in

That was David's pebble felling Goliath to the ground. Lajuninais ended by making the counter-motion, that during the legislative period and for three years after the close of it, no representative of the nation be allowed to accept from the executive power any place, pension, preferment, grace, etc.

Mirabeau's reply was absolutely crushing, but he spoke against a pre-determined and irrevocable resolution. Nobody so much as attempted to answer him; he was simply voted down.

"I cannot believe that the author of the motion seriously wishes to have determined that the *élite* of the nation cannot contain a good minister.

"That the confidence accorded by the nation to a citizen must be a reason for excluding the confidence of the king. . . .

"That in declaring that, without any other distinction than that of virtues and talents, all citizens have an equal aptitude for every employ, one must except from that aptitude and that equality of rights the twelve hundred deputies honored by the suffrage of a great people.

"That the National Assembly and the cabinet

the *Archives Parlementaires* is so brief, that it is worthless. Not even any allusion is made to this sentence.

must be so divided, so opposed to each other, that one ought to discard all means which might establish more intimacy, more confidence, more unity in the plans and in the measures.

"No, gentlemen, I do not believe that this is the object of the motion, for I shall never be able to believe an absurdity.

"Nor can I imagine that what with our neighbors serves the public welfare, can be with us only a source of evils. . . .

"Nor can I believe that it is intended to offer this insult to the cabinet, to think that whoever belongs to it must *eo ipso* for this fact be suspicious to the National Assembly.

[1] "To three ministers already taken from the midst of this Assembly and almost upon its vote, that this example has taught that a similar promotion would be dangerous in the future.

"To every member of this Assembly that, if he were called into the cabinet for having done his duty as citizen, he would cease to do it by the fact in itself of his being minister. . . .

"I besides ask myself: is it a point of the con-

---

[1] The reader has of course to supply for this and for the following sentence, "to offer this insult", from the preceding paragraph.

stitution one proposes to settle? The moment has not yet come to examine whether the functions of ministers are incompatible with the quality of representative of the nation, and such a question cannot be decided without discussing it at length.

"Is it a simple police rule which one intends to establish? Then there is perhaps a previous law which one ought to obey, that of our mandates, without which none of us would be what he is; and in this respect one ought, perhaps, to examine, whether this Assembly is competent to establish for this session an incompatibility of which the mandates know nothing and to which no deputy has subjected himself.

"Shall every representative be forbidden to resign? Our liberty would be violated.

"Shall he who resigns be prevented from accepting a place in the cabinet? Then one intends to curtail the liberty of the executive power.

"Is it proposed to deprive the constituents of the right to re-elect the deputy whom the king has called into his council? Then not a rule of police is to be rendered, but a point of the constitution must be established."

"Furthermore: can it not easily happen that

the Assembly itself believes salvation dependent on having ministers, that share its principles and views, taken from its midst?

"However great the number of statesmen, which so enlightened a nation as ours may contain, is it nothing to render 1,200 citizens ineligible, who already are the *élite* of the nation?

"I ask: shall the king prefer courtiers or those to whom the nation has not given its confidence, though they may have solicited it, to the deputies of his people?"

As it is impossible to answer these questions, he says, it is impossible that the ostensible object of the motion be its true purpose. "To render homage to the intentions of him who has moved it, I am forced to think that some secret motive justifies it, and I shall try to divine it.

"I believe that it can be useful to prevent certain members of the Assembly from entering the cabinet.

"But as it is not proper to sacrifice a great principle in order to obtain this specific advantage, I propose as an amendment the exclusion from the cabinet of those members of the Assembly whom the author of the motion seems to fear, and I undertake to name them.

"There can be, gentlemen, but two members in the Assembly, who can be the secret objects of the motion. The others have given sufficient proofs of liberty, courage, and public spirit . . . Who are these members? You have already guessed it, gentlemen; it is either the author of the motion, or myself. . . The amendment, gentlemen, which I propose, is, that the exclusion which one demands, be confined to M. de Mirabeau, deputy of the commoners of Aix."

One would have to search the annals of parliamentarism a long time to find another speech every single sentence of which is such a sledgehammer stroke. Never did a prouder word pass the lips of Mirabeau than his amendment, and it painted the situation with photographic exactness. The vanquished put himself the laurel wreath of victory upon his brow, and the victors stood before him as culprits caught in the act. Blin's motion, to exclude the members of the Assembly for the duration of its session from the cabinet, was adopted by a great majority, but the Assembly had borne testimony to the immense superiority of the man and its unappeasable jealousy of him in a way, which put an indelible stigma not only upon its political discernment, but also upon its patriotism.

"Every time that Mirabeau was too much in the right," says Méjan, the editor of his speeches, "he was accused of having too much talent"; and, "they only assassinated the principles and reason." Alas! they did more. They also ground the axe for Louis XVI., and at the crank of the whetstone stood those who palmed themselves off as his only trusty knights. Most of the "right," *i. e.*, the conservatives, voted with the dominating faction of the majority for Blin's motion, and La Marck directly charges Cicé with being the real originator of the plot which was hatched against Mirabeau and his motion between the two meetings of the Assembly on the 6th and 7th of November.[1] Led by a minister of the king, his especial champions stabbed the one man who could have saved him, if it still was possible to save him,[2] and therefore they stabbed the king by stabbing Mirabeau.

[1] Corresp., I. 420–422. Lafayette corroborates La Marck's assertion.

[2] I cannot refrain from calling attention to the following remarkable sentence in a letter written by Mirabeau on Sept. 3, 1788—notice the date—to his uncle: "Un évenement (his election to the States-General) qui me mettrait en scène dans un moment qui va recommencer la monarchie, en la constituent, *si elle est encore susceptible d'être constituée.*"—Mém., V. 193. The italics are mine.

"I should think myself very happy if, at the price of my exclusion, I could preserve to this Assembly the hope to see several of its members, worthy of my confidence and all my respect, become the confidential advisers of the nation and the king, whom I shall not cease to consider indivisible." With these words Mirabeau had concluded his reply to Lajuinais. They were not a hollow and hypocritical phrase, but expressed his true sentiments. Though he ardently wished to become himself minister, not only to satisfy his burning ambition, but also because he was thoroughly convinced that as a statesman he towered far above all others, yet he deemed the legal establishment of the correct principle concerning the relations of the two departments of infinitely greater import than this or any other personal question. This is no mere conjecture: the assertion is fully provable by positive evidence.[1]

[1] On the 18th of November he writes to his sister Mme du Saillant : " Ne me parle pas de ces haines trop bêtes si elles ne sont pas atroces, et ne t'en fâche pas pour nous, mais pour le bien de l'Etat, et de la révolution qu'ils ne comprennent pas ; en vérité j'aurais le droit d'en parler comme Cicéron à Atticus." Allusion is made to the passage in the 16th letter of the 1st book, commencing : " Quaeris deinceps, qui nunc sit status rerum, et qui meus."—Mémoires, VI. 420.

The second list of ministers in his handwriting, which I mentioned, does not contain his name, and Lafayette states directly: "Mirabeau renounces entering (the cabinet), provided that he has an influence upon it."[1] Then he (Mirabeau) again and again repeats—as well in his private correspondence as, at a later period, in his Notes to the court—that there is no salvation, unless the insane decree of November 7th be repealed, and in these declarations his own name is, at the most, mentioned, so to speak, incidentally; as a rule they contain no reference whatever to himself. Thus he writes already at the end of 1789: "What more will have to be done?—Revive the executive power; regenerate the royal authority, and conciliate it with national liberty. That will not be done without a new cabinet, and this enterprise is noble and difficult enough for one to wish to belong to it. But a new cabinet will always be badly composed, so long as the ministers are not members of the legislature. The decree concerning the ministers must therefore be reconsidered. It will be reconsidered, or the revolution will never be consolidated."[2]

The brief but masterly recapitulation of his

[1] Mémoires, II. 432. [2] Corresp., I. 429.

reasons for this opinion in a Note of the 12th of September, 1790, to the court, is so absolutely free from personal considerations that, so far as this is concerned, it might have been written by a Washington. The decree, he says, " must be openly attacked by the king and by all those who want to save at the same time the monarchical government and the kingdom," for, " in a representative government it is impossible that the ministers should not sit in the legislative body, if the nation is not to be exposed to violent shocks and the royal authority to continual attacks. Their presence alone can serve there as an intermediary and common bond between the powers, which it is easier to separate in theory than in practice. Thereby all the active measures of the legislative body will seem measures of the executive power; one would no longer present two opposite ends to the respect of the people; there would be unity of action in the authority; the National Assembly would increase its real strength; and the king would preserve his prerogative. If this measure is always indispensable in the form of government which we have adopted, it is still more so in a moment of revolution, when the royal authority, assaulted on all sides and paralyzed in all its energies, can perish either by inaction or by the rivalry of another authority, which would only need to be favored by circumstances to crowd it out entirely."[1]

That was but too true, because when it had been decided that the king was to have only a "suspensive" and not an absolute veto, the question of granting him the right of dissolving the legislature was, as M. Loménie says, "considered as *ipso facto* discarded."[2] Without the possibility of appealing from the legislature to the people, and the ministers "being mere clerks (*commis*) at the Assembly's commands,"[3] the crown was completely at its mercy.

The fatal seed yielded, month after month, a more abundant crop of poisonous fruit. Mirabeau's anxiety to find some means of uprooting it, therefore, steadily increased, though the realization of his wish to enter the cabinet himself palpably became more and more impossible. In October, 1790, he repeatedly advises the king, if the decree be rescinded, either to appoint a mixed cabinet—half moderates and half radicals—or to give all the places to pure Jacobins. The first proposition was based upon what he had written

[1] Corresp., II. 178.   [2] Ib., IV. 438.   [3] Ib., V. 16.

half a year before to Lafayette in proposing to him an alliance once more: let us "unite the opinions by the men, as we cannot unite the men by the opinions."[1] The latter advice is in itself irrefutable proof that, apart from all personal aims and ends, he implicitly believed what he said about the absolute necessity of an organic connection between the legislative and executive power. But there was, unquestionably, also more than a grain of truth in his oft-quoted remark: "Jacobins that are ministers will not be Jacobin ministers."[2]

It hardly needs to be stated that when in September, before the fall of Necker, he advised the king openly to attack the decree, he intended to do so himself. We have the draft of the speech he proposed to deliver in the Assembly.[3] "He aban-

[1] Apr. 28, 1790. Corresp., II. 4. [2] Ib., II. 228.
[3] Mémoires, VIII. 126–149. "Voilà où nous a conduit la séparation inconséquente des premiers agens du pouvoir exécutif et des réprésentans de la nation. Oui, je suis forcé de le répéter, les malheurs qui ont accompagné les premiers temps de notre révolution, ceux dont nous avons été successivement assaillis jusqu'ici, ceux dont nous sommes menacés encore, n'ont eu et ne pourront avoir de cause plus directe et plus certaine . . . je vais tâcher de vous démontrer, par une analyze exacte et rigoureuse, que pour l'avenir comme pour le passé votre décret serait une cause essentiellement génératrice d'anarchie et de discorde, car il est tout-à-fait

doned the intention, because he soon became convinced that there was not the slightest chance of success, and without the possibility of success the attempt would have been a gross, tactical blunder, for it could only have the effect of lessening his influence and furnishing arms to his enemies. Lafayette cut the string of his bow.

As early as the summer of 1789 Mirabeau had told the Assembly: "You must show a profound contempt for the absurd dogma of political infallibility."[1] The admonition was as little heeded as most of his warnings. The further the Assembly advanced in its revolutionary course, the more it became addicted to the sweet sin. Its worst offspring was the resolution that its decrees should be irrevocable, until a new constituent Assembly was convened. The doubts as to the wisdom of this course were, however, after all, not completely silenced. At least a back-door was provided to remove rotten timber if it should appear that by

---

destructif de la constitution dont l'établissement vous occupe :

1. Parce qu'il porte atteinte au droit de la nation ;

2. Parce qu'il empêche l'accomplissement du premier devoir du monarque ; et parce qu'il gêne, dans l'exercise des leurs, et les ministres et l'Assemblée.

[1] Aug. 18. Œuvres, II. 36.

some inexplicable accident the infallible builders of the New France had used any. Neither the next legislature nor the people were to have any power over their work, but they themselves were to revise it before attaching to it the unbreakable seal of legal infallibility. This opportunity Mirabeau was to improve, though, as he said, "It was mounting the breach and exposing myself to great dangers." Trusting that public opinion in the provinces would give him sufficient support, he was determined "openly to attack all that part of its (the Assembly's) work, which is the cause of the present calamities of the kingdom ... leaving it no alternative but complete retraction or stubborn obstinacy." He was confident that, if properly managed, the disgust of the departments with "the legal anarchy" could be turned to such account, that a "counter-revolution in the idea" would be "as inevitable as invincible." "Lafayette," he writes, "at first entered upon this plan and undertook to have the materials collected; soon he saw in it only a means to separate the constitutional from the regulative articles, to fill up some gaps in the actual constitution and to elude the imperious and salutary necessity of a ratifying assembly. Then he wanted to charge a committee with this labor, though it cannot be divided . . . ; he was sure, he said, that he could get me into that committee and have me made its reporter. Finally . . . he resolved to concert with the Jacobins the success of a plan which the Jacobins had to fear the most. He believed that he could re-establish the principles of the monarchical government by the influence of a republican sect." The committee was appointed, and Mirabeau was not made a member of it, though, as he asserts, Lafayette had the day before, given "his word of honor" to another person that he would be.

As to this last charge, Mirabeau himself or his informant has probably laid the color on too thick. Thus much, however, is certain. Lafayette, who emphatically disclaimed any republican tendencies, who ever posed as the especial champion of the constitutional monarchy[1]—Lafayette, who had

[1] At least in his professions towards the king. What he really was—a monarchist or a republican—it is impossible to tell, simply because he never knew it himself, being also in this respect "l'homme aux indécisions." He declared himself to have been in 1789 at heart a republican, but by necessity a monarchist. On the 27th of March, 1793, he wrote from Magdeburg to Mr. Von Archenholz in Hamburg : " J'avais sacrifié des inclinations républicaines aux circonstances et à la volonté de la nation."—Mém. de Dumouriez, II. 459.

forsaken Mirabeau in the decisive battle of the 7th of November, now rendered the decisive defeat of that day irretrievable. "Finding a board that had escaped the public shipwreck," Mirabeau bitterly exclaims, "he has laid his hands on it only to break it." [1]

Then he professed to have been converted into a royalist by the events of the 5th and 6th of October, 1789. D'Estaing wrote on the 7th of October to the Queen: "M. de Lafayette m'a juré en route, et je le crois, que ces atrocités avaient fait de lui un royaliste." (Moniteur, II. 46.) On the 20th of May, 1790, he plumes himself on his royalism, and boasts of a victory over the republicans. He says, in a letter of that date, addressed to his cousin Bouillé: "Il s'est élevé dernièrement une question sur la paix et la guerre qui a séparé notre parti, d'une manière très marquée, en monarchique et républicain: nous (the former) avons été plus forts; mais cette circonstance et bien d'autres, m'ont prouvé que les amis du bien public ne sauraient trop s'unir." (Mém. de Bouillé, 123.) The flight of the king caused him to return to his old love. According to Ferrières he considered it "comme la voie la plus propre de conduire à la république." (Mém. de Ferrières, II. 334.) Nevertheless he went with the royalists. The manner in which the fact is stated by him in the above-quoted letter to von Archenholz, is certainly a corroboration rather than a denial of Ferrières's assertion. "Lorsque après son (the king's) évasion l'Assemblée constituante lui offrit de nouveau la couronne, je crus devoir reunir ma voix à la presque unanimité de ce decret."—Mém. de Dumouriez, II. 461.

[1] Corresp., I. 192-195.

LECTURE X.

Other Defeats and Mischievous Victories.

"ONE must never judge my conduct in part, neither upon one fact, nor upon one speech. Not that I refuse to give my reasons for every one; but one can only judge them as a whole and exercise an influence by the whole. It is impossible to save the state day by day." Thus wrote Mirabeau on the 10th of May, 1790, to the king.[1]

Unquestionably, in the nature of things it is impossible to save a state day by day. But it is certain that, unless he did just this, he could not save it at all, for insurmountable obstacles barred every other way against him. Though it became from week to week more true, it had been true from the beginning what he wrote in January, 1790, to La Marck: "We drift at random on the sea of unforeseen events, old prejudices, and invidious passions."[2] There was no one in com-

[1] Corresp., II. 13.   [2] Ib., I. 446.

mand of the craft. It ploughed its way through the surging waves, as the fitful storm happened to strike the sails. We have seen how Mirabeau had tried to avert this by urging the legal captain actually to assume the command and keep the vessel upon a predetermined course. He had failed, and from the first hour everything concurred to render it from day to day more certain that every attempt, either to set a captain over the crew or to have a definite course laid out, must result in a more complete failure. To do this, would by no means have rendered salvation a certainty; but without doing this, salvation was no more possible than a house can be built without a base on which to build. From time to time and in regard to this or that question, Mirabeau might succeed in preventing a fresh blunder or even in getting the right thing done; but all he could thereby achieve was at best that the vessel would keep afloat a little longer. At best, for what was in itself an achievement would always be liable to be turned into a fresh source of calamity by adopting only one half of his advice and rejecting the other half, while its salutariness depended altogether on its adoption as an integral whole.

The father compared Mirabeau's mind to a mirror, in which everything is pictured and effaced in an instant. Loménie endorses[1] this harsh judgment and finds its justification, as to his policy, principally in its innumerable and rapid mutations.[2] So far as the charge is borne out by the facts, it serves as a proof of Mirabeau's claim to genuine statesmanship.[3] If he had not displayed such a versatility in his tactics and even in his strategy, he would have been what Loménie believes him to have been: an orator with a rather thin and pretty impure varnish of statecraft. One of the main charges he brought against Necker was that

---

[1] IV. 73, 74.

[2] If the charge is true, then no man was ever guilty of grosser self-deception than he. He wrote to Mauvillon: " J'ai mis plus de suite qu'un autre mortel quelconque, peut-être, à vouloir opérer, améliorer et étendre une révolution qui, plus qu'aucune autre, avancera l'espèce humaine. Vous verrez aussi que ce qui n'a dû vous paraître longtemps que les aperçus électriques d'une tête très-active, était la combinaison d'un énergique philantrope, qui a su tourner à son but toutes les chances, toutes les circonstances, tous les hasards d'une vie singulièrement étrange, et féconda en bizarreries et en singularités."—Lettres à Mauvillon, 476.

[3] He writes, January 4, 1790: " Les cartes sont tellement mêlée dans ce tripot-ci. il est si difficile pour un joueur un peu systématique d'y combiner un coup, les sottises de part et d'autre y déjouent si complètement tous les calculs, qu' après une déperdition d'esprit et d'activité, dont chaque journée est très-fatiguée, on se retrouve au même point, c'est-à-dire au centre du chaos."—Corresp., 447.

the minister was in his policy "always at war with the circumstances."[1] He was not guilty of the same mistake, for he understood that the statesman has to shape his policy according to the circumstances, though he be ever so much displeased with them. He never changed as to the What, and not to change as to the How would have been the height of impotent doctrinarianism, because the circumstances were constantly undergoing such changes, so that to-day was worthless or worse than worthless, what some weeks or months before had been best calculated to attain the What. No consistency as to ways, means, and methods was possible, so long as wind and waves had virtually sole command of the ship. So long as this was the case, the true statesman could have but one aim and end: to get her out of this condition at any risk; for as long as she was in it, everything else was necessarily but a hazardous makeshift. And to get her out of this condition was Mirabeau's one aim and end, and became so ever more and more, the more it became evident that the task could not be accomplished. On this question everything depended, and as to this question, his very victories had necessarily the effect of defeats.

[1] Corresp., II. 155.

Necessarily, for it was but too true what he wrote to Lafayette: "The circumstances are very great, but the men are very small." [1] They were not quite so small as they appeared to him in his wrath, but still they were too small to see how small they were as to statecraft in comparison to him. They realized the difference just enough to resent it most bitterly. The thought to have the state saved by him was so unbearable to them, that it rendered them incapable of honestly examining the question, whether it could be saved without him or not. Whenever his ascendency approached a certain line, they deemed it a sacred duty towards themselves and the country to thwart him without stopping to ask, whether they thereby did not thwart themselves and drag the country further towards the brink of the abyss. His only source of power was his genius, and that was a blade without a handle and a lever without a fulcrum, if those, who alone could make his thoughts authoritative, active will, were determined under no circumstances to do so to the

---

[1] Dec. 1, 1789. Corresp., I. 423. To Mauvillon he wrote: "Helas! mon ami, vous avez trop raison: *Beaucoup de vanité et peu d'amour de la gloire.* C'est à cause de cela qu'il faut changer le caractère national."—Lettres à Mauvillon, 507.

extent it had to be done, if it was to be of avail.

On the 7th of November the Assembly had chained itself down to this determination by erecting it into a law; and the one man, with whose aid the wheels could perhaps, after all, have been reversed, was quite as effectually chained down to it by political shortsightedness, misplaced moral punctiliousness, and, above all, the jealousy of unbounded petty vanity.

Circumstances had lifted Lafayette into such a position, that it may be considered doubtful whether Mirabeau could have sufficiently fructified a victory on the 7th of November, if he did not succeed in either conciliating or overthrowing him. But the defeat was unquestionably irretrievable if he could do neither. From the 5th of October, Lafayette was the most powerful man in the realm, not to do good, but to avert as well as to bring about some of the worst evils. Therefore one of the main points in Mirabeau's programme from that day on is to coax or to force him into an offensive and defensive alliance, or to break his power. The unintermitted and most arduous struggle to achieve either of these ends is a continuous series of defeats, and next to that of the

7th of November he has suffered no more portentous ones.

Mirabeau always lent a helping hand to his adversaries. In this case, too, he was far from being blameless. Lafayette's character renders it a certainty that he could never have made up his mind to accept in thorough good faith the proffered alliance. But Mirabeau made it doubly certain by airing most freely his contempt of the general's political capacities, and by indulging in regard to him too in his dangerous taste for inventing nettling sobriquets. That the caps fitted the general's head to perfection was not calculated to make him fancy them any better, and the balm of fulsome flattery, which Mirabeau now and then poured over the wounds, could not have much healing effect, because the perfume of insincerity was too strong.

Upon Lafayette, however, rests by far the greater half of the responsibility that this alliance was not concluded, which might have changed the fate of France. Though the idea of it was profoundly distasteful to Mirabeau, because the mean opinion he had of the general's talents rendered it humiliating to him, he repeatedly returned to the charge, because he was equally well aware that the chance of overthrowing him was exceedingly small, and that the imperative interests of the country admitted of no other alternative than an alliance. And coarse flattery was not the only means by which he tried to attain his end. He did address him also as a man, whose better and higher impulses ought to be considered as so strong, that they can be successfully appealed to in the language of bitter, but wholesome truth. If Lafayette's character had been of that loftiness of which he himself was ever the last man to entertain the least doubt,[1] resentment would not have

---

[1] His self-complacency and self-deception verge upon the comical. The most perfect of men cannot rightfully claim "la tranquillité d'une conscience pure qui n'eut jamais à rougir d'un seul de ses sentiments, ni d'une seule de ses actions." The man who approaches the nearest to this angelic purity—frail human nature being left out of his moral make-up—will be the last to speak and boast of it. Lafayette was ever the herald of his own virtues, and in sounding their praises he opened his mouth as wide as a public crier. "Je vous jure," he wrote in June, 1789, "que dans les douze ans de ma vie publique, si j'ai fait beaucoup de fautes, je n'ai pas eu un moment dont je ne m'applaudisse, et parmi les fautes que j'ai faites il y en a beaucoup que je dois à la prudence d'autrui." Happy France! Things were being set to rights by this immaculate man, into whose ears even the whisperings of ambition tried to worm their way in vain. In a letter to the Duc de Liancourt, which must have been written in the second half of August, 1789, he says: "Ma situation est bien étrange. Je suis dans une grande

been the principal and ultimate effect of Mirabeau's castigations, accompanied, as they were, by earnest entreaties. He would have confessed to himself that he, too, was indeed far from being spotless, and in the consciousness of his own shortcomings he would have found the moral courage to silence the protests of his self-righteous virtuousness, and for the country's sake to lock arms with the giant, though, as a contemporary says, his face was punctured not only by the small-pox, but also by vice. More than once Lafayette was on the point of doing it, but at the last moment the promptings of his nobler qualities were always overcome by the insinuating sophisms of his smaller self. And he not only drew back, but he drew back in a way which proved that even as to fundamental principles, his virtue was not entirely flawless. "Let M. de Lafayette name a single occasion when I have not done more than I had promised him; *let him name a single one, when he has not failed to keep his word with me*, and I consent to declare our accounts

avanture, et je jouis de penser que j'en sortirai, sans avoir eu même un mouvement ambitieux à me reprocher, et après avoir mis tout le monde à sa place, je me retirerai avec le quart de la fortune que j'avais en entrant dans le monde."—Mém. de Lafayette, I. 307, 272, 276; édit. 1837-39.

balanced."[1] On the 3d of October, 1790, Mirabeau charged La Marck to send this message by Ségur to Lafayette, and neither the general, nor Ségur, nor any of his other friends has ever been able to refute the accusation that he repeatedly did go back upon his solemn engagements with Mirabeau.

Nobody will contend that the moral repulsion, with which Lafayette tried to justify his conduct towards Mirabeau,[2] was either feigned or without cause. But unless Lafayette knew of a hand equally skilful and strong, he could neither as a statesman nor as a patriot justify his pushing away this one because there were some ugly stains on it. And he never even pretended that he knew of such a hand, except his own, and history gives, no doubt, full answer to the question, how far that was equal to the task. Besides, how could a candid man, who felt such an unconquerable moral repulsion, write to the object of this moral repulsion: " Mutual confidence and friendship, that is what I

---

[1] Corresp., II. 208. La Marck writes Nov. 9, 1790, to Mercy-Argenteau: "sa (Lafayette's) mauvaise foi égale son incapacité." Ib., II., 300.

[2] "Lafayette eut des torts avec Mirabeau, dont l'immortalité le choquait . . . il ne pouvait s'empêcher de lui témoigner une mésestime qui le blessait . . . On craignit mes répugnances pour son immoralité."—Mémoires du Général Lafayette, II. 367.

give and expect."[1] No, not the moral repulsion, but something else was really unconquerable.

Lafayette writes in his Memoirs in regard to Mirabeau's wish to be elected President of the Assembly for the " Federation " festival of July 14, 1790 : " Lafayette, without offering any opposition to his being President on another occasion, wished for this one a virtuous patriot, and he said so frankly." Now, either Mirabeau deserved the unconquerable moral repulsion, and then he was never worthy to occupy the chair of the Assembly, or he was, his moral taints notwithstanding, worthy to occupy the chair of the Assembly, and then the unconquerable moral repulsion overshot the mark. But, apart from this, Lafayette's nice distinction would have been plausible, if the occasion had been simply a patriotic festival without any political import, and if Mirabeau had merely intended to serve some personal ends. The general was, however, aware that neither was the case. He knew that Mirabeau wanted to improve the unique

---

[1] Corresp., I. 413. Oct. 29, 1789. It is besides deserving of notice that according to his own confession the moral scales he himself used in politics were none too sensitive. He writes : " Je me suis souvent servi d'instruments qu'il faudra bientôt briser. J'ai tout essayé excepté la guerre civile."—Mém., I. 272 ; edit. 1837-39.

opportunity to blow the dying embers of loyalty into a flame, which might have given again some solidity to the breaking rivets of the tottering throne. And this opportunity Lafayette would not let him have, not because he was illoyal, not because he was consciously striving for a republic, but because he himself wanted to cut the most prominent figure on the occasion—because he wanted to be, what Mirabeau declared him to be, "the rival" of the king.[1] And if he wanted to outshine the king, the thought that he might be outshone by Mirabeau was, of course, utterly unbearable to him. These are not conjectures. His vanity was too great to allow him to refrain from proclaiming it with his own lips in a most offensive manner. When Frochot asked him his reasons for objecting to Mirabeau alone as President, he replied: "Mirabeau behaves too badly towards me; I have vanquished the King of England in his power, the King of France in his authority, the people in its fury; I shall certainly not yield the place to Mirabeau."[2] "These words show," remarked Mirabeau, "how far he is possessed of the secret of his smallness and the weight of his vanity." Indeed, a crushing weight. Vanity is to

[1] Corresp., II. 26.   [2] Ib., II. 54.

such a degree the dominant trait of his character
that to it more than to anything else it is due that,
apart from his American *début*, all the unparalleled
opportunities offered him by the strangest coin-
cidence of circumstances are invariably cast away,[1]
frequently even turning his good qualities and
high aspirations into direct means for inflicting
the greatest injuries upon his country. Even his
staunch friend and admirer, Jefferson, is compelled
to charge him with "a canine appetite for popularity,"[2] and Lafayette himself directly endorses
this judgment by speaking of "the delicious sen-
sation of the smile of the multitude."

But there were yet other defects in Lafayette's
intellectual and moral make-up, which rendered it

[1] Bouillé characterizes him thus: "Je redoutais son caractère méfiant et dissimulé, plus que son ambition, que
j'aurais désiré voir satisfaite, s'il avait voulu sauver le roi,
la monarchie et sa patrie, en arrêtant la révolution au point
où elle était alors (Oct., 1789), et en établissant un gouvernement sur des bases et sur des principes solides et convenables
à la France et au génie de ses peuples. M. de Lafayette le
pouvait ; il était le seul homme qui eût alors assez de force
et de puissance ; mais il avait de l'ambition, sans le caractère et le génie nécessaires pour la diriger : elle se réduisait
au désir de faire du bruit dans le monde et de faire parler
de lui. Ce n'était pas un homme méchant, et encore moins
scélérat ; mais il était au-dessous, je pense, de la grande circonstance où il se trouvait."—Mém. de Bouillé, 85.

[2] Jefferson to Madison, Jan. 30, 1787. Jefferson's Works,
II. 108.

imperative upon Mirabeau to exert himself incessantly and to the utmost to effect his overthrow, when the negotiations for an alliance came to naught. He never tires in his Notes to the Court of analyzing the reasons which must make every day another step towards perdition, so long as one does not muster courage to shake off this incubus. If he had never written anything else, these criticisms upon Lafayette's character, the nature of his power, and the inevitable consequences of the two, separately and combined, would secure him a place among the keenest and most penetrating political thinkers and observers of all times. Though La Marck is right in saying: "There are 2,000 causes for a single effect,"[1] the history of the revolution becomes surprisingly lucid, if one but fully grasps the leading facts constituting the main working causes. Among these, however, Lafayette and the nature of his power are unquestionably of the very first rank, and as to all the principal points, Mirabeau understood the man as well as his position so completely, that all the researches of history have only served to corroborate his judgment.

Ever since the 5th of October, Mirabeau calls

[1] Aug. 23, 1791. Corresp., III. 178.

him "dictator" and points out that his dictatorship is of the worst kind imaginable, because it is merely a fact and therefore uncontrolled by the consciousness of responsibility. This was all the more a danger which it was impossible to overestimate, because to this man a real dictatorship would have been as much a horror, as he delighted in this counterfeit of it. To be called and to fancy himself dictator and really to be one to the extent not only of being more powerful than any one else, but also of being indirectly[1] able to prevent everybody else from doing what he did not want to be done, that was the acme of his ambitious cravings. But though he valued this ten times more than his life, he would ten times rather risk losing it all, than formally and officially to assume the supreme direction with immortal glory at the end of the narrow and rugged path, but the spectre of perdition grinning up to him from the precipices on the left and on the right. Not only his physical courage and his own belief in the intensity and perfect honesty of his lofty sentiments and aspirations are above suspicion; as to the negative side also his moral courage must be acknowledged to have been

---

[1] By the agency of those upon whom the official responsibility rested.

of a high order. But as to the positive moral courage, which in mighty political and social upheavals is the most indispensable requisite of a man in a leading position, he was most lamentably deficient. In the garb of extreme favor fate was, in fact, very cruel to him, for it thrust him into a first-class rôle, and the essential elements for sustaining in such times the part of a *character* was entirely forgotten by nature in his intellectual and moral equipment.

On the 28th of April, Mirabeau wrote to Lafayette: "In the midst of so many dangers I forget the greatest: the inaction of the only man who could prevent them. But, undoubtedly, this dictatorship is not to consist in doing nothing."[1] No, not exactly, but, as I already intimated, worse than that: his doings were confined to preventing others from doing what ought to have been done. This he did most effectually, for, as La Marck said: "Insufficient in the great things, this man is very adroit in the small ones."[2] One would, however, do him wrong by supposing that his barring the way to others was entirely due to the irrepressible jealousy of his vanity. To a great extent it sprang from the same cause that was at the bottom of his

[1] Corresp., II. 3.   [2] Ib., II. 285.

doing nothing himself. Mirabeau calls him
"*l'homme aux indécisions*, the man of indecisions.[1]
He ever at the same time wills and wills not, never
willing so clearly and so resolutely that he feels it
to be an imperative necessity and peremptory *duty*
to act up to his will. The more momentous the
question, the surer it is that he will either try to get
off with the semblance of acting, or come to a dead
halt in his acting, ere it becomes decisive. "Decision," however, as Mirabeau told him, "is what we
need the most and the only means of salvation."
And, like all men who lack this quality, he tried
to make up for his own deficiency by consulting
other people to such an extent that bad was rendered worse—especially as he took good care to
ask advice only where he was sure that the answer
would not be wholly distasteful. To his face
Mirabeau severely reproved him for his proneness
to surround himself exclusively with men who,
though not without merit in some respects, are
after all only second and third class and utterly
unfit for the tasks to be performed, because "not

[1] Corresp., II. 34. On the 24th of October, 1789, La Marck writes to Mirabeau : "Il est tout à fait à vous, et il le serait efficacement s'il savait, non pas être décidé, mais conserver la décision dans laquelle il est laissé chaque fois qu'on lui a parlé de vous comme j'en pense."—Corresp., I. 402.

one of them knows the men and the country, not one of them knows the affairs and the things. Marquis, our time, our revolution, our circumstances resemble in nothing what was; neither by *esprit*, nor by memory, nor by social qualities can one to-day conduct oneself; only by the combinations of meditation, the inspiration of genius, the omnipotence of character." [1]

It would be difficult to imagine a worse combination of qualities for a dictator, and the nature of Lafayette's power was such that an absolutely fatal crop of consequences had inevitably to spring from it.

Mirabeau says in his Note of June 1st, 1790, to the court: "Lafayette derives his force from the confidence which he inspires in his army (*i. e.*, the national guard of Paris). He inspires this confidence only because he seems to share the opinions of the multitude. But as it is not he who dictates these opinions—for of all cities in the kingdom it is Paris where public opinion, directed by a mass of writers and a still greater mass of other lights, is the least at the power of one man—it follows that Lafayette, who has acquired his influence only by singing to the tune of Paris, will always be forced,

[1] Corresp., II. 20.

in order to preserve it, to follow the torrent of the multitude. What barrier could he oppose to it? —Will a general of national guards not soon be without soldiers and without power, if his principles are not those of his army?—It is, therefore, easy to foresee, what his conduct will always be. To fear and flatter the people; to share its errors from hypocrisy and from interest; to sustain the most numerous party, whether it be right or wrong; to frighten the court by popular movements, which he will have concerted, or which he will cause to be apprehended in order to render himself necessary; to prefer the public opinion of Paris to that of the rest of the kingdom, because he does not derive his force from the provinces—that is the often culpable and always dangerous circle, in which he must needs be compelled to move—that is his whole destiny."

"Though not a demagogue this man will therefore be formidable to the royal power so long as the public opinion of Paris, of which he can only be the instrument, will make it a law unto him. Now supposing that the kingdom returns to sounder ideas on true liberty, the city of Paris will be the last to change principles, for it is the deepest steeped in radicalism. Therefore it is of all citizens, Lafayette, upon whom the king can count the least. . .

"What would it then mean to compose the cabinet of men devoted to Lafayette?—They would strive to make the whole kingdom conform itself to Paris, while the only means of salvation is to bring Paris to its senses by the kingdom. . . At the same time slave and despot, subject and master, he would be the most formidable tyrant."[1]

On the 15th of September, Mirabeau summed up this reasoning in a few words: "All powerful for doing harm, Lafayette is and must become more and more powerless to prevent it."[2] Five days before he had already written: "It is possible that the shame of tolerating an insurrection in the presence of an army of 30,000 men will drive Lafayette some day to fire upon the people. Well, he thereby would wound himself mortally. Would the people, who have demanded the head of M. Bouillé for having fired upon revolting soldiers, forgive the commander of the national guard after a combat of citizens against citizens?"[3] And in November, when the mob vented its wrath

[1] Corresp., II. 27-29.   [2] Ib., II. 182.
[3] Ib., II. 171.

upon the residence of M. de Castries for his having wounded in a duel Charles de Lameth, Mirabeau dryly remarked: "This man," I said to myself, "who sees this house devastated as a simple spectator, will have neither the force nor the influence, if it become necessary to save the king." [1]

Every one of these assertions has been borne out by the facts—every one of these predictions has been fulfilled to the letter.

To determine correctly the responsibility that rests upon Lafayette personally, the question must, of course, be propounded and answered, how far the vicious nature of his power resulted from circumstances over which he could exercise no control. Mirabeau did not fail to see that this was to a very considerable extent the case. If he had been heard betimes and his advice had been followed implicitly, this would have been different. It is one of the earliest and most momentous cases, in which infinite harm resulted from his achieving but half a victory.

To his motion of July 8, 1789, concerning an address against the concentration of troops, had been attached the motion, to request the king "to order that in the cities of Paris and Versailles civic

[1] Corresp., II. 341

guards be at once levied, which, under the orders of the king, will be amply sufficient to maintain public order and tranquillity."[1] An overwhelming majority voted for the address, but an overwhelming majority also adopted the amendment of Gaulthier de Biauzat to strike out all that related to the formation of civic guards. As soon as the dismissal of Necker became known in Paris, the gravity of this blunder became apparent. After the mischief was done, which Mirabeau had intended to prevent, the civic guard was organized, but in spite of the horrors which had preceded and followed the storming of the Bastille, half of his advice remained even then unheeded. In what manner he proposed to have the guard put " under the orders of the king," cannot be said to a certainty. It is, however, probable that his idea was, pursuant to a suggestion from Duroveray, to have the officers appointed by the government.[2] The government was allowed no direct influence whatever upon it, and the consequence was that the national guard, gradually but steadily, lost its original character.

[1] Œuvres, I. 308.
[2] Lafayette, on the contrary, warned the electors of Paris on the 14th of July, " de se défier des officiers généraux que le gouvernement mettrait à la tête de la milice bourgeoise."
—Procès-verbal des électeurs, I. 405.

From an instrument to maintain the government of the law, it was changed more and more into an instrument for promoting the revolution, radicalism, and, ultimately, the undisputed sway of the sovereign mob and its demagogical leaders. "One can hardly imagine," writes Mirabeau on the anniversary of the portentous victory of the Paris mob in Versailles, "how much the petty vanity to be armed, to have a uniform, to play at soldier, to make oneself noticeable, to obtain a command, and, above all, a kind of impunity, have contributed towards rendering the French heads revolutionary."[1] And in the great Memoir of December, 1790, he declares that, "in an infinite number of respects the national guard of Paris" is to be considered "an obstacle to the re-establishment of order. Most of its chiefs are members of the Jacobins, and, carrying the principles of this society among their soldiers, they teach them to obey the people as the paramount authority. This troop is too numerous to acquire a corps spirit; too closely connected with the citizens ever to dare to resist them; too strong to leave the smallest chance to the royal authority; too weak to oppose itself to a great insurrection; too easily corrupted,

[1] Corresp., II. 243.

not in the aggregate, but individually, not to be an instrument ever ready to the hands of the factions; too conspicuous by its apparent discipline not to give the tone to the other national guards of the kingdom, with which its chief has the infatuation to correspond; finally, too ambitious not to render the formation of a military household of the king very difficult."[1] Here again the history of the revolution is a running commentary upon his assertions, fully bearing out every one of them. The national guard, which, if organized before the storming of the Bastille and upon sound principles, might have done so much towards awakening, propagating, and enforcing a proper understanding of true liberty, became indeed one of the main obstacles to the re-establishment of order, because, as with its chief, the power for doing mischief increased as fast as that of preventing it diminished. There was only this difference in the two cases, that his race was run much sooner than that of the national guard. When his eyes were partly opened to the fact, where he had helped to lead the country, and when he earnestly, though with no more political discernment and positive courage than before, tried to reverse the wheels,

[1] Corresp., II. 418.

the national guard just entered upon that phase of its downward evolution, which commenced by its being the conscious and willing ally of the rabble, and ended by its being itself the organized rabble.

To understand fully the import of this portentous evolution, it must be borne in mind that at the time France had virtually no army. "Since it has learned the public law, the army is no longer an army," Mirabeau wrote to La Marck a few days after the mob had forced the king to transfer his residence to Paris.[1] As early as the 8th of July he had warned the government that this would be the effect of " electrifying ' the troops ' by the contact with the capital and interesting them in our political discussions."[2] The National Assembly was not slow to endorse the reproofs administered to the government, but it had no ear for the equally emphatic warning that this was at least as great a danger to the liberty it proposed to establish, as to the crown. Soon, however, this became so apparent that it passed a formal vote of thanks to Bouillé, when he argued the question with the rebellious regiments at Nancy with powder and lead. But though in an emergency the Assembly still mustered sufficient courage to eulogize some-

[1] Oct. 16, 1789. Corresp., I. 383. [2] Œuvres, I. 304.

body else for daring to do the right thing, it was much too faint-hearted to draw itself the logical conclusions of the fact that as it was told by Mirabeau, " with an army without discipline public peace cannot exist."¹ It did not want to understand that, as a little water is but fuel to a great fire, " special decrees for every particular insurrection" were worse than worthless. How could the systematic and heroic cure proposed by Mirabeau —disbanding of the whole army for the purpose of reorganizing it at once upon the basis of an adequate oath—meet with any favor in an Assembly, which accompanied with demonstrations of displeasure his declaration that, to counteract the ill use made by the people of the rights of man, a declaration of the duties of every citizen had become necessary!

In the address of the 9th of July he had made the Assembly say: " Sire, we are always ready to obey you, because you command in the name of the laws . . . our very fidelity orders us to resist," if your agents were to do violence to the laws.² This was sound doctrine in a state that proposed to establish a government of law. But it was a most monstrous doctrine, if it was virtually inter-

¹ Œuvres, IV. 10.   ² Ib., I. 315.

preted to the effect that only the king and his agents should be bound by the laws. In theory and in practice the people and their representatives had to be as implicitly subject to them, and this was, in the nature of things, impossible to attain, unless the laws entrusted to the government the means required for executing the laws. Every month this was more lost sight of, by the people as well as by the Assembly. As the revolution recognized the people as the source of the law, the logic of the masses, armed with the rights of man as the supreme law, concluded that they, in their quality of people, were superior to the law; and the Assembly, though not formally and expressly endorsing this claim as the Convention was to do, rendered the complete realization of the doctrine inevitable, by acting upon the principle that to establish liberty the government must above all be debarred from being a government. "Take care" —Mirabeau warned them in the debate on the right of peace and war—"take care that, by carrying the distrust of the moment into the future (*i. e.*, the constitution), we do not render the remedies worse than the evils. . . Take care that, in order to restrain (the government), you do not render it incapable of acting. . . Take care; we would confound all powers by confounding action with will, direction with law; the executive power would soon be only the agent of a committee; we would not only make the laws, but also govern."[1]

As to the particular question in hand, he carried his point in the main, as I have mentioned before: as to the general question he was, according to his own testimony, utterly defeated. The National Assembly, he says in the Memoir of December, 1790, "has believed to solve the problem of a perfectly free monarchy, by creating a royalty without power, without action, without influence, admitting it in theory, and forgetting it in practice."[2] This has been done, as he asserts,[3] because " the secret object of the legislators was to organize the kingdom in such a manner that they would have the option between republic and monarchy—" " the materials for a republic greatly exceeding those

___

[1] Œuvres, III. 334, 335, 337. In the same debate he said: " Prétendez-vous, parce que la royauté a des dangers, nous faire renoncer aux avantages de la royauté. Dites-le nettement: alors ce sera à nous déterminer si, parce que le feu brûle, nous devons nous priver de la chaleur de la lumière que nous empruntons de lui. Tout peut se soutenir, excepté l'inconséquence: dites-nous qu'il ne faut pas de roi, ne nous dites pas qu'il ne faut qu'un roi impuissant, inutile."— Œuvres, III. 374.

[2] Corresp., II. 442. [3] Oct. 14, 1790. Corresp., II. 226.

for a monarchy," as he declares in November.[1] But, as the Assembly has " established a kind of democracy without destroying the monarchical government, or rendered royalty useless without establishing a complete democracy, *i. e.*, has abandoned its original basis without putting anything in the place of it," this has resulted in the formation of "a monstrous government, which it is impossible to put into effect;"[2] therefore the constitution would only have to be left to itself to render " its self-destruction almost inevitable."[3] The intended organization of a monarchy with the monarch practically left out, he insists, has resulted in the construction of a nondescript commonwealth without any executive. " The Assembly, while admitting royalty, has not erected an executive power. I do not intend merely to say that it has arrogated this power to itself. I mean that it does not exist, and even cannot exist."[4]

If any one thing is more irrefutably established by the subsequent course of events than another, it is the truth of these charges. But if this is so, was Mirabeau then not egregiously mistaken when he wrote to his uncle in October, 1789, that the

[1] Corresp., II. 320.
 Ib., II. 215.
[2] Ib., II. 432.
[4] Ib., II. 427.

revolution necessarily had " to go a hundred times further than one could have imagined," because after the storming of the Bastille " one no longer thought of establishing liberty, believing that it had been conquered?"[1] Indeed, no! This *was* one of the main roots of the whole disastrous development. On the 14th of July everything had yet to be done as to the *establishing* of liberty. Up to that day, and by that day, nothing was achieved but the absolute certainty, that by the government and the reactionists of the two upper orders any effectual resistance to the establishment of liberty could no more be offered. The Assembly, however, thought exactly the contrary, or at least acted as if it thought the reverse. It deemed liberty conquered, *i. e.*, established, and saw its task in rendering impossible its being ever again wrenched from the people by the government and the upper orders. Mirabeau, on the contrary, saw with the utmost clearness that these quarters were now completely at the mercy of the victorious revolution, and that henceforth the real danger lay exactly in the opposite direction. " You," he told the Assembly in his great speech of May 22, 1790, " you only speak of checking the ministerial

[1] Loménie, V. 421.

abuses, and I talk to you of the means to repress the abuses of a representative assembly. I talk to you of arresting the insensible inclination of every government towards the dominant form, which one impresses upon it." [1] Here is the real danger, because a numerous assembly " cannot be subjected to any kind of responsibility." [2]

From this point of view, he had in September, 1789, so strenuously and persistently fought for the royal veto, not, as he declared, as a royal prerogative to which the king had an inherent claim, but because required by the public welfare as a bulwark for the people against their representatives.[3] If these were sustained by the people,

[1] Œuvres, III. 365.

[2] "On parle du frein de l'opinion publique pour les représentans de la nation ; mais l'opinion publique, souvent égarée, même par des sentiments dignes d'éloges, ne servira qu'à la séduire : mais l'opinion publique ne va pas atteindre séparément chaque membre d'une grande assemblée."—Œuvres, III. 320.

[3] "Si quelque traces de précipitation et d'immaturité marquaient déjà l'avenue législative où elle (la nation) est entrée, conviendrait-il de n'environner les législateurs d'aucune barrière ; de ne leur opposer qu'une résistance de forme qui s'évanouit d'elle-même ; de leur livrer ainsi sans défense le sort du trône et de la nation ?

"Les sages démocraties se sont limitées elles-mêmes ; elles se sont défendues par des précautions puissantes contre la légèreté des actes publics ; les lois qu'elles se donnent sont élaborées successivement dans différentes chambres, qui en the king would anyway always have "to obey." But, if there arises a difference of opinion between the perpetual representative of the people, the king, and its temporary representatives as to what the interests of the state require, it is proper and necessary that by means of the royal veto the question be submitted to the people for adjudication.[1] Lafayette persuaded Montmorin and Necker to declare on the part of the government that the king would be satisfied with a suspensive veto. That was, as experience taught, ten times

examinent les rapports, les convenances, le fond et la forme; ce n'est que dans leur parfaite maturité qu'elles sont portées à la sanction populaire. A plus forte raison, dans une monarchie où les fonctions du pouvoir législatif, celles-là même qui ont le plus d'activité, sont confiées à une Assemblée représentative, la nation doit-elle être jalouse de la modérer de l'assujettir à des formes sévères, et de prémunir sa propre liberté contre les atteintes et la dégénération d'un tel pouvoir ; car il ne faut pas l'oublier, l'Assemblée nationale n'est pas la nation, et toute assemblée particulière porte avec elle des germes d'aristocratie.

"Quelles précautions ont-elles été prises, dans la constitution qui se prépare, pour garantir la nation ce ces dangers? Nous voyons le pouvoir exécutif surveillé, contenu de toute manière ; et nous ne connaissons jusqu'à present d'autre règle au pouvoir législatif que ses propres lumières, d'autres barrières que sa propre volonté. En se constituant corps unique, il est privé de l'avantage de se contrôler lui-même, et de mûrir dans son sein ses propres délibérations." Nouveau coup d'œil sur la sanction royale.—Mém. VI. 443, 444.

[1] Œuvres. II. 93, 96, 99, 100, 114.

worse than no veto power at all would have been, for while it did not give the king the power, which Mirabeau demanded for him in the interest of the people, it compelled him to make himself personally the target of the unbridled passions and sinister demagogy.

But not the king alone had to pay dearly for Mirabeau's defeat. The history of the veto question is one of the strongest proofs that the Assembly was the victim of a gross delusion in believing, that to break down the power of the executive was identical with increasing and confirming its own power. With Lafayette, the ministers, and the Assembly, the decisive argument was the wrath of Paris. Not the Assembly, but the clamor of the unreasoning masses instigated by irresponsible agitators, virtually decided the question. The Assembly was already far on the highroad towards rendering " the legislator himself," as Mirabeau said, " nothing but a slave, who is obeyed when he pleases, and will be dethroned, if he shock the impulse which he has given." [1]

In this case the government, the commander-in-chief of the national guard, the Assembly, and the people had united in breaking the shield, with

[1] Corresp., II. 445.

which Mirabeau tried to protect at the same time the king, the Assembly, and the people. In other questions of equal import he was compelled in a way to lead them himself, with open eyes, towards the precipice.

Thus, above all, in regard to the assignats. It is as undeniable that to him more than to any one else it was due that the Assembly attempted by this means to avert bankruptcy, as it is certain that among the levers, with which France was precipitated into the abyss of terror, this device was one of the most powerful. To acknowledge this is, however, by no means to admit that the responsibility for its having this effect rests upon him. "To-day bankruptcy, hideous bankruptcy is there; it threatens to consume you, your prosperity, your honor—and you deliberate!"[1] Thus Mirabeau closed his wonderful improvisation for instantly voting the extraordinary income tax of 25 per cent, demanded by the government, and the vast hall seemed to shake under the convulsive applause elicited by the overpowering fervor of his patriotic appeal.[2] Was bankruptcy afterwards

---

[1] Œuvres, II. 187.

[2] In a sense it hardly can be called an improvisation. Nearly two years before, in a letter addressed to Montmorin

less hideous, less dangerous? Did the facts not prove with really terrible impressiveness that this one word contained, as he asserted, all calamities, all horrors, that of national dishonor included? And if so, was it then not right, nay an imperative duty to have recourse to assignats, although he knew them to be a seed, which might be eventually turned into dragon teeth? Yes, he knew that full well. Although he saw and laid stress upon the fact that the assignats were most effective weapons against the enemies of the revolution, because whoever owned an assignat had a personal interest in upholding it,[1] he avowed that the measure had at first "frightened" him,[2] and in his 28th Note to the Court he wrote: "Can one guarantee the success of the assignats? I answer frankly, no. One can guarantee nothing in a kingdom like France, and above all in circumstances, when so many different passions and so

(Nov. 20. 1787), he had hurled as withering denunciations against bankruptcy contemplated at the time by the government as a means to obviate the necessity of calling the States-General. " Deshonorés au dehors, furieux au dedans, en dérision aux autres, en horreur à nous-mêmes, dangereux seulement à nos chefs, tels nous allons être, si le roi montre seulement l'intention de manquer à ses engagements." See the whole letter.—Mém. IV. 468–477.

[1] Œuvres, IV. 61, 78.   [2] Ib., IV. 50.

many prejudices are engaged in perpetual combats."[1] But on the other hand he again and again insists that one is in the vice of stern necessity—that there is no choice.[2] And neither then nor ever afterwards has a single one of those, who have condemned him, been able to refute this assertion or even but attempted to say, what else could have been done. Nor is there, so far as he is concerned, any force whatever in the argument that, while bankruptcy would have been a terrible calamity in 1789 and 1790, it became a hundredfold more terrible calamity by being staved off for some years by means of the assignats. The fact is undeniable, but he cannot with any color of justice be held responsible for it. No man in the Assembly had a fuller and correcter conception of the overshadowing importance of the financial question, and therefore also no man insisted earlier, more strenuously, and more persistently, upon its being treated in a comprehensive and systematic way.[3] But he preached to deaf ears. He compared the emission of assignats to the treatment of skilful physicians who, though they

---

[1] Corresp., II. 155.
[2] Œuvres, IV. 83, 84, 85, 122, 123, 178.
[3] Ib., III. 86, 87.

do not cure, prolong life by fighting the most immediate cause of danger, and thereby procure a chance for the healing forces of nature to assert themselves.[1] The Assembly acted as if it deemed the emission of assignats the financial salvation of the state. He said: "The interregnum of the laws is the reign of anarchy."[2] The Assembly, in a hundred ways, protracted and aggravated the interregnum of the laws. He, conforming himself to the ever-changing circumstances, devised means after means that could be made conducive to a condition of things, which would render it possible to improve the prolongation of life attained by the assignats to initiate by political sanitation the gradual economical sanitation. The Assembly not only refused to do whatever would have made them fit means for a great end, but it and its successors directly perverted them into a most efficacious means to thwart his ultimate end: the reestablishment of a real government. To hold him responsible for the mischief wrought by the assignats has about as much sense as to charge the crimes of the Inquisition to the teachings of Christ.

Was he equally blameless as to the equally per-

[1] Œuvres, IV. 76. [2] Ib., IV. 28.

nicious consequences of his half-victories in the church question? It is certainly impossible to prove it, and even to make it plausible would be a very hard task. He saw from the first that the Assembly, in taking up the question in the manner it did, inflicted a wound upon the revolution so deep and so malignant, that it might easily prove fatal; and his later systematic efforts to entangle the Assembly more inextricably in the suicidal policy, were a part of his general plan to discredit it for the purpose of opening a way to a wholesome reaction.[1] For these two facts there is positive and irrefutable proof in abundance, and they go far towards proving that his guilt cannot be as great as it appears at first sight. But they are surely not sufficient to exonerate him completely.

[1] Corresp., II. 365, 366, 367, ff. He writes, Jan. 27, 1791 : "Voilà une plaie toute nouvelle, mais la plus envenimée de toutes, qui va ajouter encore un foyer de gangrène à tous ceux qui rongent, corrodent et dissolvent le corps politique ; nous nous étions fait un roi-effigie, sans pouvoir : et un corps législatif qui administre, qui informe, qui juge, qui récompense, qui punit, qui fait tout, excepté ce qu'il doit faire. A présent nous arrangeons, le schisme religieux à côté du schisme politique ; nous n'avions pas assez de résistance, nous en suscitons à plaisir : de dangers, nous évoquons le pire de tous ; d'embarras, nous soulevons le plus inextricable : c'est de quoi amener la fin de tout, si l'Assemblée ne se lasse pas bientôt d'obéir aux anarchistes."—Mém. VIII. 248.

To determine with exactness the extent of his guilt is, however, impossible, because we are not fully informed about his motives. There is still a veil spread over this important chapter of his revolutionary career, and it will, perhaps, never be removed. To me it seems likely that here, as according to his own confessions in many another case, the excitement of the moment and the provocations of the injudicious stubborn resistance of the adversaries of the revolution, lashed his impetuous temper into such a passion that, ere he was himself aware of it, he had rushed far beyond the line which, in his own calmer judgment, he ought not to have overstepped. However that be, thus much is certain, that his course in this question raised a barrier between him and the king, which the character and the religious views of Louis XVI. rendered more insurmountable than any other, and this was as great a calamity for France as some of the worst blunders of the Assembly. The unbreakable chains, which a fatal concatenation of uncontrollable circumstances fastens to the arms of the giant of the revolution, are riveted by his own guilt.

LECTURE XI.

Mirabeau and the Court.

EVER since unimpeachable documentary evidence was brought to light, proving that Mirabeau was for a long time the secret adviser of the court, innumerable persons in France and elsewhere have deemed this fact in itself incontestable proof, that he was a double-faced and double-tongued wretch —a paragon of the vilest type of traitors, betraying equally both parties they pretend to serve. Mirabeau himself in July, 1790, when suffering from an attack of the disease which ended his days a few months later, sent to La Marck his papers, including the notes to the court, requesting him " in case of death to give them to some one taking enough interest in my memory to defend it." In reply to La Marck's answer accepting the trust, he wrote: " I assure you that my courage is greatly revived by the thought that a man like you will not suffer that I be entirely misjudged. I shall either soon go hence, or I shall leave in your hands noble elements of vindication." [1] Now, whatever else Mirabeau may have been, an idiot he was not. It is, therefore, patent, that either those must be guilty of an absurdity, who consider him convicted of revolting depravity by the fact in itself of his having entertained clandestine relations with the court, or that his moral vision must have been so abnormal that he, in good faith, mistook black for white. A moment's reflection ought to convince any one, that not the moral, but the historical vision of those severe judges is most strangely obfuscated.

France was engaged in a revolution, but whoever intimated that this revolution was anti-monarchical, was at the time universally hooted down as a base calumniator. But if the revolution was not intended to be anti-monarchical, how then could it be incompatible to be at the same time a sincere revolutionist and the adviser of the crown? As to Mirabeau it is manifestly nonsensical to assert such an incompatibility, for we have heard him declare before the States-General met, that he was determined to be "very monarchical." He simply was true to his word. The fact in

[1] Corresp., I. 23.

itself, that he acted as adviser of the crown, does not cast a shadow of a shadow upon him. That, however, is not saying that he was blameless. But whether he was guilty and, if so, what the character and the extent of his guilt was, depends entirely on the answers that must be given to the following two questions: what were his motives for advising the court, and what advice did he give? Or to put them into a more definite form: was he a mercenary and a recreant to the political convictions he still publicly professed? The two questions cannot be separated. To form an intelligent opinion and judge fairly, all the facts constituting the case and having a bearing upon it, must be known and considered in their connection as a whole.

Mirabeau received money from the king. That is an established fact. An equally undeniable fact, however, is, that for generations public opinion —and more especially that of the upper classes— considered it a matter of course, that anybody who had a chance to get money from the king should improve it. If we want to be just judges, we must keep this well in mind, because Mirabeau, like every historical personage, has to be judged by the standard of his and not of our times.

Mercy d'Argenteau, the Austrian ambassador, and La Marck were men not only of spotless, but of most scrupulous honor, and while they were perfectly familiar with the laxity of Mirabeau's moral principles in money and other questions, the thought never entered their heads that the fact of his taking money from Louis XVI. could in the opinion of any one throw the slightest reflection upon him. Nor were they altogether wrong, even if he be weighed on the more sensitive scales of our times, for he was paid for work done and services rendered. And the work was not only very considerable, but it also involved no small outlay for paying collaborators, agents, clerks. If Mirabeau had received nothing, he would have given not only his time, but also his money to the king. That was not only more than anybody had a right to expect from him; he could not have done it for the simple reason that he had no money. It is true: by the death of his father he had become the legal owner of a fair fortune, though the old Marquis had made his second son the principal heir—the legal owner of a fair fortune, but he had by no means come also into actual possession of it. The great economist had left his affairs in such a tangled condition, that unless Mirabeau withdrew entirely from politics and devoted himself for some time wholly to his private interests, he remained exactly in his former condition, *i. e.*, a bankrupt with such a mountain of debts on his back, that he had constantly all the trouble in the world to find to-day the money he absolutely needed for the morrow. For nearly a year longer he submitted to this, rather than to think for a moment of setting his own affairs to rights and letting the state take care of itself. That at all events proves that hankering after money was not the dominant trait of his character. The trouble was, in fact, that now as ever before, he was wholly destitute of a proper appreciation of it. In a sense he cared no more for it than for the dirt under his feet. That, money or no money, he was to gratify his every desire, was to him a matter of course. He, therefore, always spent lavishly—his own money, if he happened to have any, if he had none, that of other people. It may sound strange, and still it was so; money was no object at all with him:[1] all he cared about was, without having to think of money, always to do what could not be done with-

[1] See the characteristic story told by Mme. de Nehra. Mem. IV. 419, 420.

out having plenty of money. He was therefore sorrily unscrupulous about how he got the money he wanted to spend, but for the same reason he also never even felt so much as tempted to stoop to means by which he would have lowered himself in his own eyes.[1] When he had written a denunciation of the Banque de Saint-Charles, he was offered a big sum for suppressing the pamphlet; he preferred to carry all he had to the Mont-de-Piété, the public pawning shop of Paris.[2] Now his creditors, whom La Marck justly calls "his worst enemies," harassed him so, that he was com-

---

[1] He was pelted by such a shower of charges of venality, that he wrote, with felicitous irony : " En vérité, je me vends à tant de gens, que je ne comprends pas comment je n'ai pas encore acquis la monarchie universelle."—Lettres à Mauvillon, 472.

[2] Corresp., I. 103. See his letter of Oct. 4, 1788, to his father. Mémoires, IV. 188–191 : " Provoqué par Dupont lui-même, que j'en atteste, bafoué par lui de ne m'être pas fait 40,000 fr. de rente dans les vertiges de l'agiotage, je suis resté étranger à toute spéculation, même innocente ; j'ai vécu, petitement vécu, de mon travail et du secours de mes amis ; mais je n'ai jamais ni joué un écu, ni reçu un sou en présent, moi qui faisait fléchir, en quelque sorte, à mon gré, le balancier de la Bourse ; moi dont on aurait payé le silence de tout l'or que j'aurais voulu accepter. . . Tant que M. de Calonne n'a pas été chef de parti et de parti dans l'agiotage, il a trouvé cela très-bien, et m'a même lancé . . . Quand le ministre a été agioteur, il a voulu m'imposer silence, et j'en ai parlé plus haut."

pletely at his wits' ends, and might have been ultimately driven to some desperate resolution, if this friend had not responded to his appeal for help in his dire distress, and yet, as La Marck says, " he would only have needed to let the gold come to him, which the factions scattered about in profusion." [1] The extravagant joy to which Mirabeau gave demonstrative expression upon learning that the king's liberality far exceeded what he had dared to hope for, was more than undignified: it was revolting. But his circumstances were such, that to say he ought not to have taken money from the king, is to say he ought not to have assumed the task he did assume. This task, however, was the attempt to save the king and the kingdom. To abandon them to their fate would certainly not have been patriotic, and I suppose that the moralists who, with the zest of holy monks burning a heretic, have nailed his memory to the pillory for taking this money, will admit that patriotism ought also to be an article in a statesman's code of morals.

But if Mirabeau consented to be the secret adviser of the court for the sake of earning the money, his vindication can, of course, not be based upon the plea of patriotism, even if one be of opin-

[1] Corresp., I. 137.

ion that his counsels were in conformity with the true interests of the monarch as well as of the state. It can, however, be proved beyond the possibility of contradiction, that the salary he received was but an incident, and not his end. Neither when he offered his assistance to the ministers before the meeting of the States-General and in the first weeks of the session, nor when, in the Memoir of the 15th of October, he urged his advice and his help directly upon the royal family, had he intimated the expectation of any pecuniary remuneration. In his negotiations with Lafayette, as we have seen, this question had indeed played no small part, because he was driven into a corner; but although he was fairly hunted down by his creditors, he had ultimately rejected the offers of the ministers and of Lafayette—the latter evidently counting upon the civil list of the king to make good his promises. After the defeat of the 7th of November, Mirabeau had been for a while in connection with the Count de Provence, pursuing the idea of making him the ostensible "pilot" with a view to being himself, under his name, the real commander. Also in this episode no mercenary motives can be proved.[1] He had soon to give up

[1] True, Etienne Dumont in his *Souvenirs* (230) asserts:

the project, because it became too apparent that the prince, though intellectually greatly the superior of his brother the king, was, as to character, wholly unfit for the part Mirabeau intended him to play.[1] After this attempt had failed, he did not again offer his services. Understood by no one and repulsed with insulting superciliousness by all whom he wanted to save, he became equally

---

"*Monsieur* s'engageait à lui payer 20,000 francs par mois jusqu'à ce que ses affaires fussent liquidées, et à devenir son seul créancier." I cannot attribute any weight to this testimony. In my opinion, the man who knows of no better way to convince the world of his superior genius than to write a big book in every way disparaging his dead friend, is a witness less to be trusted than an avowed enemy. There is no reason to suppose that Mirabeau would have made Dumont his confidant, if he had concluded such a bargain, and what we know from La Marck about his pecuniary embarrassments at the time proves, that he cannot have been a pensioner of the prince. This also disposes of the promise of the prince, published in Lafayette's Memoirs, to become Mirabeau's sole creditor. Let us take the word of the editors for it that the original is in the prince's own handwriting. Does that prove that Mirabeau accepted his offer? Neither would Mirabeau have been practically a beggar at this time, nor would the relations between the two men have been of such short duration, if a bargain of this kind had been struck.

[1] On the 23d of Dec., 1789, Mirabeau writes: "Au Luxembourg (the residence of the prince), on a peur d'avoir peur." Six days later: "Il a la pureté d'un enfant, mais il en a la faiblesse." And on the 27th of Jan., 1790: "Ce qui est au-dessous de tout, c'est *Monsieur*."—Corresp., 436, 440, 460.

embittered and discouraged. In the Assembly he spoke but seldom and in his letters he repeatedly complained of being tired and feeling bored. He, who had thus far always taken the initiative, had no hand in bringing about the change in his relations to the court. He was even wholly unaware that a change was contemplated, until he was informed that on the part of the court it was a fixed resolution.

In March, 1790, La Marck, who since the middle of December was in Belgium, received an invitation from Count Mercy to return to Paris on account of matters of importance. He at once complied, arriving in Paris on the 16th. His first interview with Mercy took place on the 18th. He expected to be interrogated on the Belgian affairs. Mercy, however, forthwith began to speak of his relations to Mirabeau and ended by requesting him to serve as mediator between the king and the great tribune. La Marck consented under the condition that Mercy should himself see Mirabeau and take part in the negotiations. As Mercy could not divest himself of his quality of Austrian ambassador he, very naturally, was loath to do so. In consequence of this difficulty the matter was allowed to rest for a fortnight. A second interview in the beginning of April resulted in Mercy's consenting secretly to meet Mirabeau in La Marck's house. The conversation ran entirely upon the political situation of France, but Mirabeau was given no intimation as to the ultimate purpose of his friend and the ambassador. Mercy, highly pleased with Mirabeau, told La Marck in leaving, that the queen wished to see him the next day. Marie Antoinette, who at the end of September or in the first days of October, 1789, had told La Marck: "I trust we shall never be so unfortunate as to be reduced to the painful extremity of having recourse to Mirabeau,"[1] now commenced the conversation by informing him, that for two months the king and she had been thinking of entering into connection with Mirabeau. After a while they were joined by the king and it was agreed, that La Marck should broach the subject to Mirabeau and invite him to submit his views on it in writing to the king. Mirabeau received the overtures with a transport of delight. The idea, as La Marck says, "to be at last enabled to be useful to the king," elated him so highly that, carried away by his sanguine temperament, the fearful obstacles in his way were, for the moment, dwarfed

[1] Corresp., I. 107.

almost into insignificance. In a letter, dated May 10th and addressed to the king, he gave, briefly and succinctly, as he himself terms it, "the profession of faith which the king has desired," declaring: "This writing will forever be either my judgment or my witness." This letter was for some time in the hands of the king, and as yet not a word had been said about money either by Mirabeau, or to him, or even between La Marck and Mercy. Mirabeau had bound himself in a way which, as La Marck justly says, " was to stake his head," without knowing whether they intended to give him a copper for it. Is that the way a man acts who means to sell himself and whose political and general conscience is in his pocket? The first to speak of money were the queen and the king, after telling La Marck that the letter of May 10th was wholly satisfactory to them, and from Mercy came the suggestion to pay his debts, in order to enable him to give his time entirely, and without being molested by his creditors, to the great affairs of state. When La Marck asked Mirabeau, to give him the figure of his debts, he very characteristically replied that he knew nothing about it, and when he had ascertained that they amounted to 208,000*l*, he dolefully said, that the king could never think of paying so much. Louis engaged to do that, paid him beside 6,000*l* a month for his current expenses, and gave to La Marck four promissory notes, each for 250,000*l*, to be paid after the close of the National Assembly, in case Mirabeau had been true to his promises.

What were these promises and how were they kept? If Mirabeau's accusers can convict him in regard to these two questions, it can, of course, avail him but little that as to the money question, he was by far not as black as they would make one believe. On the other hand, if they cannot make out a case against him in regard to these two questions, it is evident that, though his relations with the court were surely not altogether free from blame, his own opinion of them must be in the main correct. Would it be surprising if that should be the result of an impartial examination of the facts? If any man was not disposed to judge him too leniently it was Lafayette, and even he did him the justice to testify: "Mirabeau was not inaccessible to money, but for no amount would he have sustained an opinion that would have destroyed liberty and dishonored his mind."[1] If I were asked, what chapter of his whole history

[1] Mémoires, II. 367.

redounds, upon the whole, the most to his honor, not only as a statesman, but also as a man, I should unhesitatingly answer: that of his relations to the court.

The "profession of faith"[1] is preceded by the declaration, that his repugnance to playing farther an active part would be invincible, " if I were not convinced, that the restoration of the legitimate authority of the king is the first need of France and the only means to save her." The sight of constantly growing anarchy, horror at the idea of having "contributed only to a vast demolition, and the fear to see another chief of the state than the king," imperiously bid him not to stay shut up " in the silence of contempt." Whatever else the king might have to expect from his secret counsellor, he certainly did not propose to mince matters, but to be terribly plain-spoken. Or was it but the cheap trick of an audacious political juggler to tell the king to his face that nothing less than his crown was at stake? Did he intend to excite exaggerated fears in order to make his services in averting them appear much greater than they really were? The last sentences of the letter will answer this question in no uncertain way.

[1] See the letter of May 10th.—Corresp., II. 11-13.

The profession of faith itself is compressed into a single sentence: " I engage myself to serve with all my influence the true interests of the king; and in order not to have this promise appear too vague, I declare that I believe a counter-revolution as dangerous and criminal, as I deem chimerical the hope or the project of any government in France without a chief, invested with all the necessary power to apply all the public force to the execution of the law." Another sentence expresses the same idea in other words: " I am as profoundly averse to a counter-revolution as to the excesses to which the revolution, fallen into the hands of bungling and perverse men, has conducted the people." Supposing, for argument's sake, that the king and the queen wanted him to assist them in re-establishing the royal absolutism, could they, after reading these lines, still believe that they had addressed themselves to the right man? Surely, to declare the very idea of a counter-revolution "criminal," was a strange way of signifying one's willingness to become a traitor to the revolution. Mirabeau's accusers have ever deemed it superfluous to show wherein his counsels to the king were a betrayal of his political past, because to them the assertion of compatibility between faithfulness to the revolution and serving the king is a self-evident absurdity: they see in it a contradiction in terms. Mirabeau was of exactly the opposite opinion. Because he was determined to be faithful to the revolution, he accepted the king's invitation and promised to serve him. In his very first Note to the court he expressly declared, that by doing so he did not shift his position by a hair's-breadth. "I shall be what I always have been : the defender of the monarchical power regulated by the laws, and the apostle of liberty guaranteed by the monarchical power."[1]

That was not merely the announcement that he would never turn traitor to the revolution. It was the formal declaration that he was not to be expected to become in any respect or to any extent a tool. He promised to serve the king, but he explicitly forewarned him that he would never become his servant—never be at his orders. "I know," he says in his 36th Note (October 24, 1790), defending himself against reproaches occasioned by the attitude he had assumed in regard to a certain question, "I know that I have promised everything, but have I promised anything but to serve according to my principles? Shall

[1] Corresp., II. 25.

I deceive in order to please, or render myself useless in order to be faithful?"[1] Faithful, as the court seemed to understand faithfulness. True faithfulness required him to serve only according to his principles, no matter how much this might displease the court. As early as the 27th of January, 1790, at the time of his relations to the Count de Provence, he had written to La Marck: "When they have not followed a single one of my advices, not improved a single one of my conquests, not turned to profit a single one of my operations, they complain, say that I have changed nothing in their position, that one cannot count very much upon me, and all that because I do not ruin myself with a light heart in order to sustain advices, things, and men, whose success would inevitably ruin them."[2]

Even if he had intended and promised to serve the king primarily for his own sake, that would have been the only course consistent with the task he had assumed, for the whole agreement was based upon the idea of the superiority of his political judgment: he was to guide, and not to go as he was bid. But he had, in fact, consented to serve the king, because he wanted to serve

[1] Corresp., II. 265. [2] Ib., I. 460.

royalty, and royalty he wanted to serve, because he was convinced that to do so was to serve France. The court possibly still considered the three things identical, in the sense that the proper criterion for the true interests of royalty and of France was what the king deemed to be his interest. If so, the fault was not Mirabeau's. As early as December 29, 1789, he had written to La Marck: "Only one thing is clear: they would like to find for their service amphibious beings who, with the talent of a man, have the mind of a lackey. They will irremediably be ruined by having fear of men and carrying always the petty repugnances and fragile attractions of another order of things into this, where what is strongest is not yet strong enough; and where even if they were themselves very strong, they would still need, for the sake of public opinion, to surround themselves with strong people."[1] The man, whom his just indignation over the political imbecility, which frustrated all his exertions, drove to the excess of calling the king and queen "royal cattle" (*bétail*),[2] would certainly not prostitute his talent and his manhood to the extent of playing the part of a lackey. On the 4th of December, 1790, he told the king:

[1] Corresp., I. 441. [2] Ib., II. 237.

"The question is no longer merely to save royalty, but to save the public cause and the kingdom."[1] To make this distinction was to announce that, if —by the fault of the king or without it—an incompatibility between serving the king and saving the public cause and the state should arise, he would no longer be found at his side. In the Memoir of the 15th of October, he had already declared this most explicitly and emphatically, directly to the royal family, and according to his radical friend Cabanis, he repeated this declaration shortly before his death in regard to the same eventuality, the flight of the king to the frontier, substituting, however, for the "denunciation" of which he had given notice in the Memoir, the announcement that he would "cause the throne to be declared vacant and the republic proclaimed."[2]

---

[1] Corresp., II. 382.

[2] "J'ai défendue la monarchie jusqu'au bout ; je la défends même encore que je la crois perdue, parce qu'il dépendrait du roi qu'elle ne le fût point, et que je la crois encore utile ; mais s'il part, je monte à la tribune, je fais déclarer le trône vacant et proclamer la république." (Corresp., I. 252.) La Marck insists that Mirabeau can have said no such thing, because, as we know, he declared again and again the departure of the king an absolute necessity. I see no difficulty in reconciling this fact with the statement of Cabanis. That he writes simply "departs" certainly does not preclude that Mirabeau spoke or, at least, only thought of a flight to the

To declare a counter-revolution "criminal" was absolutely devoid of sense, if he did not mean to serve the king only because and so far as the interest of the state required it. To arraign him for his relations to the court is, therefore, simply absurd, unless he can be convicted either of having changed his mind as to the criminality of a counter-revolution, or of having defined the counter-revolution, which he deemed criminal so narrowly, that achievements of the revolution were to be sacrificed, which he had hailed or even declared indispensable.

If the documents are studied, so to speak, only from the headings, it seems easy to convict him out of his own mouth of both charges. For a con-

eastern frontier with a view to invoking the aid of foreign powers. La Marck's statement, that he communicated the result of his negotiation with Bouillé to Mirabeau, and that he (Mirabeau) expressed himself satisfied with it, is also not incompatible with this opinion. The sounding of Bouillé as to his willingness to aid the king in leaving Paris did not necessarily imply just *such* a flight, and La Marck does not say, that he told Mirabeau that it was this that was contemplated. What Mirabeau says in the Memoir of the 15th of October on this question, renders it an impossibility that he should have approved of such a plan as that, which the king afterwards tried to execute. Yet on June 4th, 1790, he writes to La Marck: "Il ne faut, en aucun cas et sous aucun prétexte, être ni confident, ni complice d'une évasion, et qu'un roi ne s'en va qu'en plein jour, quand c'est pour être roi."—Corresp., II. 34.

siderable time he goes to the length of contending that even a civil war might be resorted to to bring about the necessary reaction; and the central idea of the great Memoir of December, 1790, is a thorough overhauling of the constitution and the systematic discrediting of the National Assembly, because unless it be ruined in the public estimation, the contemplated changes in the constitution cannot be effected. Thus he undeniably does advocate a counter-revolution. But if we take the pains to read the whole Memoir, and not only to read, but also to study it, we see that he after all persists in his unqualified denunciation of a counter-revolution by any illegitimate means, and, above all, by force of arms. Only in the legitimate way of revolutionizing, i. e., changing public opinion, does he want to bring about a counter-revolution. He is satisfied that this is likely, if not certain, to lead to an appeal to the *ultima ratio*.[1] But though he sets himself most resolutely against the idea of making the sword the arbiter between the king

[1] In this respect his opinions change with the changing circumstances. In the December Memoir he again assumes the possibility of attaining the end without a civil war. His principal reason for thinking that eventually a civil war would be "a blessing in disguise" was, that it "est le seul moyen de redonner des chefs aux hommes, aux partis, aux opinions."—Corresp., II. 137.

and the nation, the expectation that his policy will kindle a civil war, does not deter him from advocating it. Not the king against the nation, but the majority of the nation, headed by the king, fighting the minority, which by its factiousness and insane radicalism hurries France into perdition—that is the civil war he has in view. Closest alliance of the king with his people and sincere identification of the king with the true spirit of the revolution—these two maxims remain to the last the main pillars on which the whole structure of his policy rests.

The December Memoir enumerates what, in his opinion, not only *ought* to be preserved of the work of the revolution, but also *will* be preserved, whatever may befall France. This list and the remarks accompanying it not only prove that he never became recreant to his original faith, but they also show that, though he passed the severest judgments upon the political incapacity of the Assembly, he never lost sight of the fact that it had done enough for France to entitle it, in spite of everything, to eternal gratitude. Of the "destructions" of the revolution, he says that "they are almost all equally beneficial to the nation and the monarch." "I mean by destructions, the abolition of all privileges, of all pecuniary exemptions, of feudalism, and of several disastrous taxes. I mean besides the destruction of the provincial bodies of the *pays d'états*, of the parliaments, of the clergy and fief-holders as political bodies in the state. I, moreover, count among the great advantages to be preserved, the uniformity in the assessment of taxes, the principles of a more popular administration, the liberty but not the impunity of the press, the liberty of religious opinions,[1] responsibility of all agents of the executive power, admissibility of all citizens to all employs, a less arbitrary way of granting favors and pecuniary aid, and a stricter control in the administration of the public funds. In a word, I admit into my system the benefits of the revolution as well as the cardinal elements of the constitution. . . In fact, I consider all the achievements of the revolution and all that must be preserved of the constitution as such irrevocable conquests that, unless the empire be dismembered, no subversion could destroy them. I even do not except an armed counter-revolution: if the kingdom be recon-

---

[1] In the Assembly he had arduously contended against mere religious tolerance, insisting that the very word tolerance implied an unwarrantable arrogation of power.

quered, the victor would, after all, have to compose with public opinion, to gain the good will of the people, to consolidate the destruction of abuses, to give the people a share in the legislative power,[1] to let it choose its administrators. From this observation I draw this important conclusion: if the advantages of the revolution and the true foundations of the constitution are indestructible, it is of little consequence whether the National Assembly suffers in its popularity, in its force, in its credit; the nation can only gain by it, because all the really useful decrees of this Assembly will survive it, and only its fall, whether it be slow or precipitate, will furnish the means to correct its work. Because this result is well assured, the true friends of liberty, those who prefer being the saviours of their country to the perfidious popularity vouchsafing them some praise, can unite their efforts to attack the Assembly, and thereby fulfill their duties as great citizens." The royal authority alone cannot even attempt the reorganizing consolidation of the true revolution, *i. e.*, the revolution confining itself to reform; only in concurrence with an Assembly of the representatives of the people, *i. e.*, in unison with the suc-

[1] "Qu'il admit le peuple à la confection de la loi."

cessor of the National Assembly, can the arduous task be accomplished.

Does this programme propose the revivification of the *ancien régime* in anything whatever? Is anything lacking in it, that is essential to a truly liberal constitutional monarchy? Is the method, by which the end is to be pursued, not that of a strictly orthodox constitutionalist?

It is neither possible nor necessary here to enter upon the details of his plan. La Marck and Mercy were full of admiration for the stupendous, all-embracing genius Mirabeau displayed in it, but at the same time they thought it too vast, too complicated, too dependent on an army of able and trusty agents whom it was impossible to find, and requiring too much time. All that was true enough. But while it is often comparatively easy to keep a leaky, storm-beaten ship afloat, if but the right thing be done at the right moment, the most skilful engineer cannot raise a sunken ship without great apparatus, the preparation and application of which is not an affair of days and weeks, but of months, if not years. That was now the condition of things. The task confronting Mirabeau was no longer to keep the ship afloat, but to raise the sunken ship. It was not due to a lack of skill or energy on his part, that she had sunk in spite of all his efforts. The hope that he would be able to save her had been revived in him by the unexpected overtures of the court, because he thought that he would now at last be put into a position to *act*. That was a gross delusion, and that he allowed himself, for a little while, to be betrayed into this delusion by the consciousness of his strength, spurred on alike by patriotism and ambition, is the one mistake which can be justly laid to his charge.

La Marck was not a genius, but a clear-headed, sober, and judicious observer. He had not hailed Mercy's communication as the dawn of morning. In his opinion they had already waited too long, and he frankly told not only Mercy, but also the king and the queen, that he greatly doubted whether Mirabeau would still be able to redress the harm he himself had helped to do. When the king announced that Mirabeau was not to be in communication with the ministers, and even enjoined the most scrupulous secrecy towards them in regard to the whole affair, the count's heart was almost as heavy as before Mercy had spoken to him. He very justly writes: "Did such means not look more like an intrigue than dexterous

and powerful measures, worthy of a government
and commensurate to the proposed end?"[1] Instead of paving the way to the concert between
the executive and legislative power, which Mirabeau deemed the primary condition for arresting
the downward course, the king, by thus giving
his relations to Mirabeau the character of an
intrigue, only paralyzed the executive still more,
by rendering unity of purpose, will, and action
more than ever impossible. The king was not
the government, and to advise the king was useless or even worse than useless, unless he persuaded or compelled the ministers to act as he
wanted them to. With a man like Louis XVI.,
the one and the other was out of the question.
If Mirabeau gained sufficient ascendency over
him, to make him not only subordinate his own
opinions to those of his counsellor, but also in a
measure to stand up for these, the ministers, if
they happened to hold different views, would only
conclude from it that an irresponsible, and therefore in a sense illegitimate, secret influence coun-
teracted the influence, which, in consequence of
their constitutional responsibility, they were not
only entitled, but in duty bound to claim; and

[1] Corresp., I. 147.

such a well-founded suspicion was certainly not calculated to foster the proper relations between them and the king. If, in conformity with the tendencies prevailing in the Assembly, they were only too much inclined to antagonize rather than to serve the crown, any manifestations of such a concealed power behind the throne would be more than likely to drive them into conscious and systematic hostility. The king's being in favor of anything would become in itself a reason for opposing it, and thus the hapless monarch would be the more in danger of turning the best advice into new sources of calamity, the more implicitly he tried to conform to it. This must be fully understood, if justice is to be done to Mirabeau in regard to his truly desperate struggle against having men devoted to Lafayette called into the cabinet. There is no answer to what he wrote October 24th to the court: "One asks of me counsels which I would give uselessly, if I cannot concert with the ministers. Whether strong or weak in fencing, I must have some ground on which to plant my foot. There are many measures, which neither the court nor I can execute, and which ministers in whom one could confide, might attempt with success and without danger.

What confidence could I have in a cabinet, created, sustained, directed by my enemy?"[1] At last a direct contact was established between him and Montmorin, that is to say, he was enabled to act through the minister, and in spite of the weakness of Montmorin's character, the connection was sufficiently fruitful to prove that in this way something might be achieved. Mirabeau virtually directed the foreign relations, and but for him the war-cloud hovering on the horizon might easily have risen then.[2]

[1] Corresp., II. 264.
[2] In the 28th Note of August 17, 1890, he writes in regard to the Spanish-English quarrel about the Nootka Sound, which threatened to drag France into a war with Great Britain : " Si vous vous êtes condamnés à un rôle passif à l'intérieur, pourquoi le ministère veut-il vous entraîner à un rôle actif à l'extérieur ? Quelle détestable politique est donc celle qui va droit à transporter sur Leurs Majestés la responsabilité qui ne peut que résulter d'une périlleuse alliance, d'une guerre désastreuse, où il n'y a pas une seule chance de succès ? Comment ose-t-on proposer au roi de tenter pour l'Espagne ce qu'il n'ose pas pour lui-même ? Comment compromet-on son existence dans une mauvaise partie qui n'est pas la sienne ?... lorsque l'anarchie est arrivée au dernier période, ne frémit-on pas à l'idée de remuer les brandons d'une querelle extérieure, qui ne peut qu'allumer une guerre générale et vingt guerres civiles dans le royaume ? Tant d'incohérence me passe, je l'avoue. Je suis stupéfait de tant de faiblesse unie à tant d'audace, et, laissant à votre habile ministère sa politique profonde, je suis trop loyal, je dois trop à Vos Majestés ce que ma conscience et mes lumières

One minister, however, was no more the government than the king was. In the main the character of Mirabeau's relations to the court remained unchanged; in some respects it even looked more than before like an intrigue on account of one minister having become a party to it. So long as every possibility was withheld from Mirabeau to bring his superior mind and, above all, his superior will directly to bear upon the government as a whole, nothing was or could be gained. He himself, as La Marck very correctly says, had been before in all essentials a strenuous defender of monarchical principles. As to himself, therefore, the court obtained by the May agreement only what it substantially had had from the beginning. In form, however, the change in his relations to the court was so radical, that to some extent inevitably even positive harm had to result from it, if in essence no corresponding change in his political position was effected. The change in form was of such a character, that it

m'indiquent comme la vérité, je suis trop avide du rétablissement de l'ordre, pour ne pas soutenir, dans le comité des affaires étrangères, que nous ne pouvons nous mêler que de nous-mêmes, et que nous ne devons chercher qu'à nous maintenir en paix avec quiconque est en paix avec nous."— To the last he remained of this opinion.

compelled him to act as if a corresponding change in essence had taken place in his position, and this not being really the case, it forced him again and again into momentary changes of attitude, injuring the court and detrimental to his influence upon it. By insisting upon its remaining a secret to the cabinet, the king had implanted an element of untruthfulness into the relation, and untruthfulness, as it rarely fails to do, yielded a rich crop of poisonous fruit.

Mirabeau never knew what the court would do with his advice, and having to act perfectly in the dark, he could not always act consistently in his double rôle of secret adviser of the king and member of the Assembly. Experience soon taught him always to expect, that from indolence, weakness, or fear, the king would ultimately do what the ministers wanted him to do. But as representative, citizen, and patriot, he was not absolved from responsibility as to what was done by telling what ought to be done. His having assumed the latter obligation had only put him under heavier bonds as to that older and paramount duty. Argument proving inefficient, he had to try compulsion, and compulsion could be exercised only by exciting fear. This he could do any moment from the tribune of the Assembly, for every day offered not only an opportunity, but also a temptation to indulge in a flight of his revolutionary eloquence. Though he well knew that this was wielding a double-edged weapon, he did it more than once, and not only when he really had no other choice. The court compelling him to have recourse to it sometimes, his hot temper betrayed him into using it oftener and striking harder with it than, according to his own confession, he ought to have done. This secret connection with the court often acted upon him more as a lash than as a curb, for, on the one hand, as La Marck wrote to Mercy, "He will not consider himself seriously engaged, so long as he only furnishes simple notes and suggests ideas which one does not follow,"[1] and on the other, he was determined to do everything in his power really to become what the king, by logical implication, had requested him to be: the directing mind and will of the government.

In January, 1791, Montmorin complained that when he spoke to the king "about his affairs and his position, it seemed as if one talked to him of things concerning the emperor of China."[2] And

[1] Corresp., II. 288.   [2] Ib., III. 30

in October, 1791, La Marck wrote: "Louis XVI. is not fit to reign—by the apathy of his character —by that rare resignation which he takes for courage and which renders him almost insensible to the danger of his position—and, finally, by that invincible repugnance to the labor of thinking, which causes him to divert every conversation, every reflection on the dangerous situation."[1] He was the same man in May, 1790, and therefore there is no doubt whatever, that he had never so much as tried to render himself an account of what his invitation to Mirabeau implied. But it is fully as certain that the king and the queen would have deemed it an absurdity as well as an indignity, if anybody had told them that it implied the request to take full charge of the helm, "It is evident," says La Marck, "that fear alone had driven them to court this formidable tribune."[2]

No one knew that better than Mirabeau himself, and he thought it best to tell his royal clients at once very plainly that he was fully aware of it. In the second Note to the court, he urges the queen to tell Lafayette, in the presence of the king: "It is evident that he (Mirabeau) does not want to help ruin us; one must not run the risk

[1] Corresp., III. 248.   [2] Ib., I. 147.

that circumstances compel him to will it; he must be for us. In order that he be for us, we must be for him. . . We are resigned or resolved to give him the confidence of despair."[1] But his object in telling this was not to increase their fear of him.[2] There was a passage in the Note, which may have impressed the queen that way; but if so, the day was to come which would undeceive her and prove that those terrible lines had not been an attempt at intimidation by a demagogue, betrayed by the impatience of his ambitious audacity into preposterous exaggeration, but the solemn warning of a genuine prophet of fearful clearness of vision. "The king," he wrote, "has but one man, and that is his wife. There is no safety for her but in the re-establishment of the royal authority. I like to believe that she would not care for her life without her crown; I am perfectly sure that she will not keep her life if she does not keep her crown." No, he does not want to sub-

[1] Corresp., II. 42.
[2] This is not mere conjecture. There is positive proof for it. He says in his 18th Note: " La dernière note que j'ai envoyée a causé de l'inquiétude, et presque de l'effroi. Je le regarderais comme un bien salutaire effroi, s'il eût produit l'activitié au lieu d'aggraver l'espèce de torpeur où réduit l'infortune. Mais comment ne pas s'apercevoir qu'en aiguisant la crainte, il émousse la volonté?"—Ib., II. 136.

jugate by intimidation. His purpose is to convince by opening the eyes to the appalling gravity of the situation, that there is but one alternative: implicit confidence or perdition. " It is no longer time either to half-confide or to half-serve. . . One must not think that one can, with the help either of accident or of combinations, get out of an extraordinary crisis by ordinary men and measures."

He read the characters but too correctly. If anything at all was to be attained, it could only be through the queen. But neither was her influence upon the king strong enough,[1] nor could she herself be made to see the things as they really were and to do with sustained resoluteness what they required to be done. While she understood better than the king the necessity of coming to terms with Mirabeau, implicit confidence was with her even more out of the question than with him. The man was repulsive to her, and while her pride was great enough to conquer fear, she had neither the keenness of intellect nor the strength of will to conquer aversion. Besides she, too, shirked the intellectual and moral effort of looking the fearful reality full in the face and pursuing her own re-

[1] Cfr. Corresp., I. 124, 125; II. 287, 288.

flections upon it unflinchingly to the end. The second time she saw La Marck in regard to the arrangement with Mirabeau, she kept him over two hours, but a great part of the time the conversation ran upon other topics. "The purpose of my audience," he says, " was almost lost sight of; she tried to turn it away. As soon as I spoke to her of the revolution she became serious and sad." But every time she soon dropped the unpleasant subject and resumed, "in a tone of cheerfulness" and with her customary "amiable and graceful humor," her sprightly chat on something else. "This trait," he adds, "paints her character better than all I could say about it."[1] Like the king she is at bottom a votary of the policy of the ostrich. Not only in her conversation, but also in her thinking does she drop the unpleasant subject when it is getting too unpleasant. Therefore she never comes to see the necessity of Mirabeau's support. When she has come to the point of admitting the necessity of conciliating him so far, that he refrains in future from putting himself at the head of the column of assault, she shudders, turns away, and deliberately closes her eyes against what lies beyond.

[1] Corresp., I. 156, 157.

This it is, above all, that from the outset dooms all the efforts of Mirabeau to utter failure. The terrific pressure of implacable cruel necessity might, perhaps, after all, have overcome the personal distrust and aversion, if king and queen had at all been capable of implicit confidence, stern thinking, whole-souled resolutions, determined, consistent, and sustained action. They themselves were the principal builders of their scaffolds, not, however, by any imputed crimes, but—to put it bluntly—by being in most extraordinary times, intellectually and morally, woefully ordinary people. They are the primary and chief authors of their doom, but infinitely less by what they do, than first by doing always the wrong thing whenever they do anything, and then by doing in the main nothing at all, never knowing either what, or when, or whether, or how to will. This is the key-note of Mirabeau's Notes. Month after month he strikes it with greater force, and finally with the fierceness of despair—ever more and more in vain.

On the 17th of August he writes: "It is time to decide between an active and a passive rôle; for the latter, though I think it wholly bad, is in my eyes less so than this alternating between attempts and resignation, half-will and despondency, which excites distrust, lets the usurpations take root, and floats from inconsistencies to inconsistencies."[1] How much effect the warning had, can be judged from the following passage in the Note of September 28th: "I confess, not without regret, that I am of very little use, but they impose upon me much more the duty to serve than they give me the possibility for doing it. They hear me with more kindness than confidence; they are more anxious to know my advice than to follow it. and above all, they do not sufficiently realize, that the passive rôle of inaction, if it were preferable to all others, does not exactly consist in doing nothing, or letting only those act who do harm."[2] On the 12th of November he writes: "The pest-laden wind, which can destroy at any moment the king, the Assembly itself, the whole nation—the secret leaven of fermentation, perpetuating and nourishing the devouring fever, are in the court; in its whole conduct, in its inaction, in its too slow or retrograde march; in its rôle of simple looker-on which it affects to play; in the perpetuity of the most detestable cabinet; in the passive system of the

[1] Corresp., II. 136.   [2] Ib., II. 196.

most bungling policy; finally, in that sum of circumstances which, persuading the feeble minds that the court has secret projects, causes the ardent minds to multiply the excessive measures of resistance. But the lightning is in the cloud."[1] By the 2d of January, 1791, he thought the court wished to get rid of him and he expressed his willingness to abandon the thankless task.[2] As early as the 17th of August he had written: " I shall wait for a clap of thunder to break this deplorable lethargy." He had waited in vain, and therefore he saw himself more and more reduced to preventing here and there, as to this or that detail, further mischief, since " Your Majesties . . . do not think yourselves in a condition to attempt anything for the public cause and yourselves." To the " silence of contempt," buoyant hope had succeeded for a moment upon the overtures of the court, because they seemed to offer an opening for at last putting the resources of his genius and the force of his will to the test of *action*, and while every day cried louder and more imperatively for action, he was, from first to last, practically condemned to talk, talk, talk—to the wind.

[1] Corresp., II. 325, 326. [2] Ib., III. 18, 19.

Even of dull Louis XVI. and merry Marie Antoinette, moulded by nature altogether for a holiday-life, it is not easy to believe that they can really have thought but for a minute, that anything could come of that. If they had, how dense must have been the film over their eyes, when they read the letter of the 10th of May! There Mirabeau had told them plainly enough how he himself viewed the prospects of the future, even if he be afforded every opportunity of making the most of all his powers in action : " I promise the king loyalty, zeal, activity, energy, and a courage of which one has perhaps no idea. I promise, in fact, everything except success which never depends on one man, and which only a very audacious and very culpable presumption could guarantee in the terrible malady that undermines the state and menaces its chief."

LECTURE XII.

The End. A Unique Tragedy.

"If this plan be carried out, one may hope for everything; and if not, if this last plank of salvation drift away, every calamity, from individual assassinations to pillage, from the downfall of the throne to the dissolution of the empire, has to be expected. What other resources can remain? Does the ferocity of the people not steadily increase? Do they not more and more foment hatred against the royal family? Do they not openly speak of a general massacre of the nobility and clergy? Is one not proscribed simply for a difference of opinion? Are the people not made to hope, that the land will be divided among them? Are not all the great cities of the kingdom in terrible perturbation? Do not the national guards preside at all the acts of popular vengeance? Do not all the magistrates tremble for their own safety, without having any means to provide for that of others? Finally, can, in the National Assembly, infatuation and fanaticism be pushed to a higher degree? Ill-fated nation! To this thou hast been brought by some men, who have supplanted talent by intrigue and conceptions by commotions. Good but feeble king! unfortunate queen! To this fearful abyss, the floating between a too blind confidence and a too exaggerated distrust have brought you! One effort is still possible, but it is the last. If it be not made—or if it fail—a shroud will cover this empire. What will then be its fate? Where will this vessel, struck by lightning and tossed by the storm, be driven to? I do not know; but if I should escape the public shipwreck, I shall always say with pride in my retreat: 'I exposed myself to destruction in order to save them all; they did not want it.'" [1]

When, in December, 1790, Mirabeau drew this appalling picture of the situation for the court, he was President of the Jacobin Club. At the time, the man holding this position had not as yet necessarily to be a conscious representative of all the subversive tendencies. The few words which Mirabeau spoke in assuming the presidency were a pointed

[1] Corresp., II. 485, 486.

rebuke of "licentiousness."[1] But the presiding over the Jacobins, after all, implied a degree of radicalism which was manifestly not in accord with his position as adviser of the court and still less with the programme of the December Memoir. From this incontestable fact, however, is not to be concluded that he plays false in the sense that he has no political convictions and no programme except, by hook or by crook, to play an important part. But it drastically shows that, his aim being what it is, the circumstances irresistibly force upon him a double part, which ultimately must defy the most consummate skill.

In his first great speech on the mines he said: "Abstractions, which are the best manner of reasoning, are neither the only nor the principal elements of the art of governing."[2] The difference between him and all the others simply consists in this, that this trite truth is fully understood by him from the beginning, that he draws all the correct conclusions from it, and that he knows what the essential ele-

[1] " Déjà tous les Français sont auxiliaires de la liberté : il ne reste qu'à les rendre tous ennemis de la licence et auxiliaires de la paix.

" C'est dans ces principes, Messieurs, que je tâcherai de remplir les devoirs de la présidence."—Nov. 30, 1790. Aulard., I. 399.

[2] March 21, 1791. Œuvres, V. 426.

ments of the art of governing are. He is fully aware that the most essential of them all is to take the people as they are, *i. e.*, that it is not sufficient to keep always in view that one has to deal not with figures and formulas but with men, but that one has besides to take into consideration the *specific* intellectual and moral conditions and dispositions of the particular nation as historically evolved and as affected by the peculiar circumstances of the time being. This intuitive political judgment, which verged upon the miraculous, was to a great extent attributable to his extraordinary knowledge of men, and this was the one good fruit of his wild and checkered career, which had brought him into intimate contact with all classes and kinds of people. The truly bewildering mobility and versatility of his own mind and temperament enabled him really to understand them all, and by his uncommon skill in asking, he improved the opportunities thus offered him in a degree no other man could have done. The Prussian Dohm writes: "He understood the art of asking in a degree of which it is hard to give a conception if one has not been present at his conversations."[1]

[1] Quoted by Professor Stern.

The art to ask pertinent questions and to ask them in such a manner that also pertinent answers are given, is, however, but one way to get at the facts, and, as I said in a former lecture, to base his policy upon the facts is the first requisite of the genuine statesman. Among the facts he has to ascertain, the frame of mind in which the people happened to be at the time in regard to the paramount questions at issue, is always one of the most important, and in a general and all-embracing revolutionary upheaval, it is by far the most essential, for the ultimate question: *what* is achievable under the given circumstances? cannot be determined, unless the correct answer is found to the question: *how* has one to set about in order to attain the end? And as to this How, the principal factor in the condition confronting the statesman is the frame of the popular mind. The most exalted statesmanship can no more ignore it in regard to the manner of proceeding, than it can overleap the limits set by it as to the What. In both cases failure is equally certain, for though there is truth in the old saying, that the great statesman does not allow himself to be dominated by the circumstances, but dominates them, circumstances can be dominated in politics only by conforming to them to a certain extent.

No statesman has ever had a higher opinion of his own powers than Mirabeau, but also no statesman has been more fully conscious of what fearful fetters those immutable political laws were to his powers. He clung tenaciously to the hope that he would ultimately succeed in spite of everything; but almost from the first it was a hope against better knowledge, for he saw but too clearly that the frame of the public mind was such as to render the case a desperate one, with, at the most, one chance against nine.

La Marck, in one of their discussions, quoted Bacon's remark, that while a little philosophy leads away from religion, much philosophy leads back to it,[1] and contended that it was applicable to almost all human institutions. "There is not one," he said, "which the shallowest declaimer could not attack with apparent success; but this success will always be annihilated by the strong reason of the ready and profound statesman, who

[1] "But farther, it is an assured truth and a conclusion of experience, that a little or superficial knowledge of philosophy may incline the mind of man to atheism, but a farther proceeding therein doth bring the mind back again to religion."—Bacon's Works, ed. Ellis & Spedding, III. 267.

knows how to defend the foundations of the social order." "Bravo! bravo!" exclaimed Mirabeau; "but that is now no longer the question. No single man will be able to bring the French back to saneness; time alone can restore order to the minds; with them one must never either presume or despair. To-day the French are ill, very ill; one must treat them cautiously."[1]

Indeed, very ill—and the nature of the disease rendered it imperative to admix a strong dose of the very virus with the remedies, so to speak, to enwrap them in it. He himself was surely one of those who, as he said, would rather save the country than enjoy "a perfidious popularity," but to dispense with popularity was in the strictest sense of the word impossible, unless he renounced the aspiration to be a determining force in the revolution.[2] Without it he was Samson shorn of his locks. In his Note of November 17th to the court he writes: "To acquire the right successfully to enter upon the course when the true interests of the throne are to be defended, it is, above all, necessary that I prepare the people to

[1] Corresp., I. 208, 209.
[2] Montmorin told him: "Vous seul avez su vous dépopulariser par courage et vous repopulariser par prudence."
—Corresp., II. 391.

hear my voice without distrust, that I dispel its suspicions, that I be counted among its surest friends, and, from this point of view, my popularity, so far from alarming the court, ought to be deemed by it its safest resource."[1] Popularity, however, could be achieved and preserved only by speaking in a tone which would awaken an echo in the breasts of the people, and, in the actual frame of the public mind, that was a tone which illy accorded with his true programme. In the garb of radicalism, often even strongly tinged with demagogism, he had to present his moderate and conservative ideas, if he were to have any chance of making them prevail.[2] Necker's celebrated daughter, Mme. de Staël, who was certainly not disposed to judge him too favorably, writes: "One could not help having pity with the constraint imposed upon his natural superiority. Constantly he was compelled in the same speech to act as partisan of popularity and of reason. He tried to wrest from the Assembly, with demagogical

[1] Corresp., II. 337.
[2] He writes Nov. 26, 1790, to La Marck in regard to his attitude in the church question: "Ce n'est qu'en se tenant dans une certaine gamme que l'on peut, au milieu de cette tumultueuse Assemblée, se donner le droit d'être raisonable." Ib., II. 361.

phrases, a monarchical decree; and he often let the royalists feel his bitterness, even when he wanted to carry one of their points; in one word, it was evident that he had constantly to combat between his judgment and the necessity of success."[1]

He had by no means a taste for such equivocal tactics. He writes to La Marck: "It makes more trouble and requires more true dexterity (not genius) thus to tack, than to fight; that is, perhaps, the rarest part of talent, at least with somewhat distinguished talents, for it is the least attractive and that which lives on little accumulated combinations, privations, and sacrifices."[2] And to the court: "One must dissimulate if one wants to supplement strength by dexterity, as one has to tack in a storm. That is one of my principles and purely based on the observation of life, for it is entirely opposed to my natural character. I must at first take the key of those whom I want gradually to force to adopt mine."[3]

It was indeed utterly opposed to his character, and therefore his skill was all the more to be admired, for he had to subject himself to no little

---

[1] Considérations sur les principaux évenemens de la révolution française, 1. 353, ed. 1820.
[2] Corresp., II. 146.   [3] Ib., II. 336.

constraint. How great this skill was, but also to what a humiliating degree he had sometimes to submit to this "tacking" policy, is most strikingly illustrated by his attitude in the debate on the important question, what the constitution should provide in regard to a regency. He is more anxious than ever to see his opinion prevail, and yet he blandly declares that he has formed no opinion; his argument is a tangle, but thus much is clear, that if it is at all intended to be indicative of what his vote is to be, he must cast it for an elective regency; he, however, abruptly breaks off and dismisses his reasoning with a contemptuous kick by declaring, in a tone of languid unconcern, that in his opinion the report of the committee, sustaining the opposite view, might be adopted. This is done, and a heavy load is taken from his mind.[1]

[1] Œuvres, V. 459–479. His true opinions are revealed by the following letter to La Marck: "Nous sommes dans un grand danger. Soyez sûr que l'on veut nous ramener aux élections, c'est à-dire à la déstruction de l'héridité; c'est-à-dire à la destruction de la monarchie. L'abbé Siéyès n'a jamais courtisé l'Assemblée, ni agioté une opinion comme il le fait, et ses partisans sont très nombreux. Je n'ai jamais été vraiment effrayé qu'aujourd'hui. Je me garderai bien de proposer demain ma théorie ; je porterai toutes mes forces à ajourner, en critiquant le projet de décret, en prouvant qu'il est insuffisant, incomplet, qu'il préjuge de grandes

Mirabeau once called the Assembly "a restive donkey, which cannot be mounted without using great discretion."[1] This time he had mounted it; but to manage the balky animal, it was, above all, necessary to keep oneself perfectly under control, and this he by no means always did. The questions, etc., etc. Certainement ma théorie ne passerait pas, et l'ajournement réussira. Envoyez chercher Pellenc (his secretary) immédiatement ; qu'il étude dans le plus grand détail le décret ; qu'il en recherche tous les dangers *pour la liberté publique ;* qu'il l'envisage sous tous les rapports : qu'il ne prenne que des notes ; mais qu'il développe assez ces notes, pour que je parle avec fécondité. Il sait au fond ma doctrine à présent, mais je ne veux que la laisser entrevoir ; je ne veux pas la hasarder ; gagnons du temps, tout est sauvé. Je crois que beaucoup de gens désirent se renfermer dans une mesure provisoire. Ne dussé-je gagner que deux jours, j'emmènerai Pellenc à la campagne avec moi, et nous y mettrons toutes nos forces. Soyez sûr, mon cher comte, que je ne m'exagère pas le danger, et qu'il est immense. O légère, et trois fois légère nation !— Notre armée est, dans cette question, pour les deux tiers à l'abbé Siéyès."—Corresp., I. 245-248. Oncken's opinion (Das Zeitalter der Revolution, etc., I. 344, 345) that Mirabeau was no longer quite in his right senses, is one of those unaccountable extravagances, with which the distinguished historian occasionally surprises his readers. He needed to remember only that the committee on the Constitution and the Assembly were not identical to find another way out of the difficulty, which, as far as he gratuitously asserts, everybody admits to be insurmountable. The wild assumption is, however, only the fitting climax of a series of one-sided and exaggerated criticisms, in which virtuous indignation has got the better of political discernment.

[1] Droz, Hist. du règne de Louis XVI., III. 59.

government and those who considered themselves the only true champions of the crown in the Assembly, vied with each other to render it almost impossible for him to do so.[1] The latter, in their passionate imbecility and blind hatred of Mirabeau, more than once succeeded in lashing him into such a fury that, while he had taken the floor for the purpose of calming and restraining, he ended by sending one revolutionary thunderbolt after the other crashing through the hall.[2]

These provocations go much further towards excusing him than it might appear at first sight, for they usually involved much more than a mere personal question, as to which he might and ought to have kept his temper. The more he wanted to keep the revolution within bounds, the

[1] "L'impéritie et la perfidie du gouvernement d'un coté, l'imbécillité et la maladresse du parti ennemi de la révolution de l'autre, m'ont entraîné plus d'une fois hors de mes propres mesures ; mais je n'ai jamais déserté le principe, lors même que j'ai été forcé d'en exaggerer l'application, et j'ai toujours désiré rester ou revenir au juste milieu."—Corresp., I. 428.

[2] See the most striking instance. Ib., II. 331.—To judge the violence of his language justly, it is, however, necessary also to keep always well in mind how true it was, what he had written already in 1787 : "Peut-on régénérer, peut-on même réformer ce pays-ci, sans attaquer aussi véhémentement les personnes que les choses?"—Première lettre du comte de Mirabeau sur l'administration de M. Necker, 7.

less he could allow anti-revolutionary ideas and tendencies to pass unchallenged. When reaction again dared to raise its voice, sound policy, his convictions, his honor, and even his personal safety made it alike imperative upon him to knock it mercilessly on the head with his terrible club.[1] But, however excusable these occasional unfeigned relapses into the tone of the radical revolutionary tribune, they had necessarily the effect of increasing every time the dislike and the

[1] In October, 1790, the question of asking the king to dismiss the cabinet and to substitute in the navy the *tricolore* for the white pennant, offered an opportunity for one of these passionate sallies. Not only the court, but also La Marck was very dissatisfied with him. Mirabeau wrote to his friend on the following day : " Hier je n'ai point été un démagogue ; j'ai été un grand citoyen, et peut-être un habile orateur. Quoi? ces stupides coquins, enivrés d'un succès de pur hasard, vous offrent tout platement la contre-révolution, et l'on croit que je ne tonnerai pas ! En verité, mon ami, je n'ai nul envie de livrer à personne mon honneur et à la cour ma tête. Si je n'étais que politique je dirais : 'J'ai besoin que ces gens-là me craignent.' Si j'etais leur homme je dirais : 'Ces gens-là ont besoin de me craindre?' Mais je suis un bon citoyen, qui aime la gloire, l'honneur et la liberté avant tout, et certes messieurs du retrograde me trouveront toujours prêt à les foudroyer. Hier j'ai pu les faire massacrer ; s'ils continuaient sur cette piste, ils me forceraient à le vouloir, ne fût-ce que pour le salut du petit nombre d'honnêtes gens entre eux. En un mot, je suis l'homme du rétablissement de l'ordre, et non d'un rétablissement de l'ancien ordre."—Corresp., II. 251.

distrust of the court. And the less the court became disposed to profit by his counsels, the more he had to be bent on strengthening his popularity. The fact that the Jacobins elected him President[1] twice in succession, bears witness to the skill he displayed in this respect. In spite of this remarkable success his position was, however, by far not as strong as it seemed. The leaders knew full well that he was the most determined, as well as the most puissant opponent of their destructive tendencies.

The political and social disintegration had by this time reached such a stage that nothing could be achieved by merely covering conservative ideas with demagogical drapery. Mirabeau had to step down to a much lower level as to his means. He frankly avows that the central idea of the great December Memoir, the systematic discrediting of the Assembly, is "an intrigue." He writes: "If the issue were not a last resource and the welfare of a great people, my character would prompt me to reject all these means of a wily (*obscure*) intrigue and insidious dissimulation, which I am forced to counsel. But what shall one do, what try . . . if one has to contend against intrigue and ambi-

[1] Each time for twenty days.

tion, and the instrument with which one is attacked is the only one with which one can defend oneself? . . . One must ruin the Assembly; the task is to save the finest empire of the world, if it still be time; such an end justifies all means, as necessity no more admits of a choice, and dissimulation, even deceit, is after all better than war.[1] And a little later: " One can only save oneself by a plan blending . . . the combinations of the statesman and the resources of intrigue, the courage of great citizens and the audacity of criminals."[2] Such was the direful situation. La Marck, whom no one can suspect of the slightest inclination to resort to means of questionable propriety, writes in the same days : " One must not overlook that we have to contend against intrigue, which almost always can be successfully met only by intrigue."[3] True enough. But to expect salvation from an intrigue was a delusion, for no intrigue could manœuvre the revolutionary tempest back into the eaves whence it had burst forth and there seal it up. The demagogical intrigues were primarily not a cause, but merely a symptom.

Nevertheless, nothing could, in fact, be done now

---

[1] Corresp., II. 463, 464. [2] Ib., II. 510.
[3] Ib., II. 416.

but to fight the devil with his own fire, for although the conflagration could not be put out, a fresh attempt to get it under control had to be preceded by beating the incendiaries off, who, systematically and with set purpose, fanned the flames and poured oil into them. Even this, however, was, under the circumstances, more than the shrewdest intriguer could accomplish. The fearful ascendency of the demagogues was due to the fact that, as Mirabeau had said, the French, *i. e.*, the whole people were " ill, very ill "—too ill not to give always ten chances to one to the intriguer for worse against the intriguer for better, provided the former had but the faintest suspicion of the latter's being astir. The intriguer, however, is surer to scent the intriguer from afar than vultures and ravens the battle-field. Mirabeau had repeatedly duped the demagogues by urging conservative measures with radical thunder, but as soon as he commenced to send Notes to the court, the pack was on his trail and never again lost it entirely. Suspicion was at times lulled, but never dispelled. Nor could it be. For as from first to last he was compelled as a rule to wear a half-mask, so also from first to last he never hesitated, when the occasion called for it, to fling it proudly away and to expose his true features in all their imposing force to the maddened radicals.

It is a redeeming feature in this checkered life, that, in his last weeks, fate offered him several opportunities to prove that he could rise to being fully his better self, growing with his opportunities morally also to his full intellectual height.

On the 1st of February, his ardent wish to preside over the Assembly was at last fulfilled, and Lafayette could convince himself that France would have been none the worse for his presiding on the day of the Federation festival. Even his adversaries had nothing but praise for him. It was universally acknowledged, that no man had presided with greater dignity and understood better to make the dignity of the Assembly respected. If such a firm and skilful hand had held the reins from the first and permanently, the Assembly would not only have worked more expeditiously and methodically, but it might have set an example as to parliamentary decorum, which would not have failed to exercise some salutary influence upon its successors and those who lorded it over them from the galleries.[1]

[1] See his graphic picture of the Assembly's haphazard way of working and the consequences of it.—Mémoires, VI. 264-266.

Only a fortnight after resuming his seat among the members, he had his fiercest encounter with the radicals and demagogues. The terrors of the revolution had driven Mesdames, the old aunts of the king, from Paris. Their passports stated that they were going to Rome. Without any warrant of law, local authorities, backed by the mob, repeatedly opposed the progress of their journey. These incidents brought the question of emigration in an acute form before the Assembly. Chapellier, speaking in the name of the committee on the constitution, proposed that a committee of three be appointed, without whose permission nobody should be allowed to emigrate. Mirabeau objected to the reading of the bill, and moved the order of the day. He insisted that it was not possible either to justify or execute a prohibition of emigration.[1] "Not indignation, reflection must make the laws," he declared. The code of Draco, but not the statutes of France, would be a fit place for a law like that contemplated by the committee. Its barbarity was the best proof of

[1] That was no new theory with him. Repeatedly and ardently he had contended for liberty in this as in all other respects. "La seule bonne loi contre les émigrations est celle que la nature a gravée dans nos cœurs."—Monarchie Prussienne, I. 20; edition in 4°.

the impracticability of any law against emigration. With the most concentrated despotism in the most ruthless hands such a law never had been executed, because in the nature of things it could not be executed. " I declare that I should consider myself released from every oath of fidelity toward those who become guilty of the infamy of appointing a dictatorial commission. . . The popularity, which I have had the honor to enjoy like others, is not a weak reed;[1] I want to sink its roots into the earth on the imperturbable basis of reason and liberty. If you make a law against emigrants, I swear that I shall never obey it." Applause and hisses interrupted the speaker at almost every sentence. The radical left grew more and more violent in its demonstrations of disapproval, until he cowed it by hurling against it, with the full force of his lion's voice, that grand, imperious: "Silence to those thirty voices!"— A motion was made and carried which virtually amounted to an adjournment of the question for an indefinite time, and as long as Mirabeau lived no law against emigration was passed.

---

[1] Méjan (Œuvres, V. 404) writes thus, and thus the sentence is always quoted. But is it not possibly a misprint, *pas* being substituted for *qu'* : "n'est qu'un faible roseau?"

Mirabeau had not achieved a victory, but merely repulsed an attack by throwing the weight of his influence and of his masterful personality to the last ounce into the scales. Whether he would be able to achieve even thus much the next time was very doubtful. Yet on the same day the radicals returned to the charge in a personal onslaught, and on the field on which the wind and the sun were always wholly with them. Reason and true liberty were by this time at a sufficient discount to warrant the hope that success would crown a vigorous effort, completely and once for all to uproot the popularity of the man whose presumptuous temerity went to the length of attempting to sink its roots into this bed-rock. The suspicion expressed by one of his admirers, that a brutal social affront was a stratagem with a view to stabbing him from behind in the back, was probably not without foundation. If so, the sorry conspirators were hoisted by their own petard: they only did him a service by giving him a warning which he did not fail to understand and to heed. He had been invited with others to dine at d'Aiguillon's. When he presented himself at the door he was refused admission. It seems to have been expected that after this slap in the face, he would not dare to show himself at the Jacobins. The "silence to the thirty voices" had reminded these heroes most forcibly, that it was certainly very much easier to slay this man with their venomous tongues when he was not there to answer them. Aye! They did not know the man yet. It had not been a vain boast, but the plain statement of a fact, when he wrote to the king: "I promise a courage of which one has perhaps as yet no idea." No surer means could have been found to make him go to the Jacobins than thus to notify him by a mortal outrage, that their leaders were determined in dead earnest to hunt him down.

We have a long and spicy report from the pen of Camille Desmoulins on this memorable evening session at the Jacobins on February 28th. Camille, once the ardent admirer of Mirabeau and his exquisite dinners, now draws his pen-picture, not with ink, but with gall and sulphuric acid. Oh, into what a pitiable and contemptible figure this reputed Titan of the revolution turns, if we but look at him closely! There he sits, writhing in impotent rage and in fear under the lash so mercilessly applied by those true giants, Duport and Alexandre Lameth. He himself had said:

"When I shake my terrible mane, nobody dares to interrupt me."[1] And now—as with Christ on Calvary, says Camille — the perspiration drips down from under his mane in large drops, pressed out by agony. And how futile his embarrassed efforts to impose upon the clear-eyed and straight-hearted patriots by his shallow sophistries, hollow excuses, and pompous oratorical flourishes! It is true: he is not ejected from the club, and when he leaves, there is some applause. But nobody is deceived. In acknowledgment of past services he is allowed one more chance to repent and return to the true faith.

Happily there is another pen-drawing of this evening session preserved, and it presents a rather different view. The Swiss Oelsner[2] also tells us what he saw with his own eyes and heard with his own ears. Full justice is done by him to Mirabeau's adversaries. In his reply to Duport, Mirabeau seems really not to have been at his best, and Lameth's onset was in fact terrible. The

---

[1] Dumont, Souvenirs, 282, 283.

[2] Bruchstücke aus den Papieren eines Augenzeugen und unparteiischen Beobachters der französischen Revolution, 1794. We owe the identification of the author to Professor Stern. I quote from Aulard's translation of the report. See the original, Stern, II. 316–319.

consummate adroitness of the attack was only surpassed by its unfathomable perfidiousness.[1] It was a master effort to render Mirabeau at the same time "odious and ridiculous." So wildly was the speaker applauded, that Oelsner began to fear that Mirabeau was done for and that nothing less was intended by his assailants than to unchain the mob against him. Perhaps it would have

[1] Already in May, 1790, Mirabeau had denounced the meanness and suicidal madness of the ever-growing practice of treating a difference of opinion as a crime and of substituting imputations and calumnies for argument. "On dirait qu'on ne peut, sans crime, avoir deux avis dans une des questions les plus délicates et les plus difficiles de l'organisation social. . .

"On vous a proposé de juger la question par le parallèle de ceux qui soutiennent l'affirmative et la négative ; on vous a dit que vous verriez d'un côté des hommes qui espèrent s'avancer dans les armées, ou parvenir à gérer les affaires étrangères ; des hommes qui sont liés avec les ministres et leur agens : de l'autre, *le citoyen paisible, vertueux, ignoré, sans ambition, qui trouve son bonheur et son existence dans le bonheur commun.*

"Je ne suivrai pas cet example. Je ne crois pas qu'il soit plus conforme aux convenances de la politique qu'aux principes de la morale, d'affiler le poignard dont on ne saurait blesser ses rivaux, sans en ressentir bientôt sur son propre sein les atteintes. Je ne crois pas que des hommes qui doivent servir la cause publique en véritables frères d'armes, aient bonne grace à se combattre en vils gladiateurs, à lutter d'imputations et d'intrigues, et non de lumières et de talens : à chercher dans la ruine et la dépression les uns des autres des coupables succès des trophées d'un jour, nuisibles à tout, et même à la gloire."—Œuvres. III. 355, 378.

come to that, if the President had succeeded in his perfidious attempt to adjourn the meeting without allowing Mirabeau once more to reply. But when Mirabeau, who, according to Oelsner, had not lost his composure for a minute, again had the floor, the conspirators had lost the game for this time. Oelsner writes: "It was a hot combat. He put forth all the resources of his genius to vanquish his young and agile adversary. He clutched him and his companions with a hand of iron and of fire. He wrenched from them their false arms and struck incurable blows. His boiling wrath gushed over all who had impugned him. Truths, which no one had ever dared to breathe in the club, crashed like claps of thunder through the hall. His boldness, his noble bearing, petrified the audience with astonishment. Thus he put down the furious, and there was not one from whom he did not force, if not applause, at least high admiration. Even in the National Assembly Mirabeau had never been more masterful."[1]

Mirabeau finished his answer to his assailants the next day in the National Assembly, as spokesman of a deputation of the departmentl adminis-

[1] Aulard, Jacobins, II. 112.

tration.¹ His attitude in the emigration question was by no means the only grievance of the Jacobins against him. One of Lameth's principal charges was, that in an address of the departmental administration to the people drawn up by him, he dared to denounce those as the real enemies of liberty, who constantly declared the constitution and liberty in danger. Mirabeau now repeated this charge more emphatically, pointing more directly to the Jacobins. "From all the fragments of the old institutions and the old abuses," he says, "an infectious sediment, a corrupting leaven has formed, which is incessantly stirred by perverse men in order to develop all its poisons. I mean the factious who, in order to subvert the constitution, persuade the people that it must act by itself, as if it were without laws, without magistrates. We shall unmask those culpable enemies of its tranquillity, and we shall teach the people that, if the most important of our functions is to watch over its safety, its post is that of labor, seconded by the peace of active industry and domestic and social virtues."² The Assembly

---

¹ In the latter half of January he had succeeded in having himself elected to the important position.
² Œuvres, V. 408.

applauded and decreed that the address be printed.

Thus ended this fierce single-handed contest with insane radicalism and ruthless demagogism, which excites even in Mr. Loménie unalloyed admiration. Mirabeau's "image," he says, "appears in it with a character of greatness," which it has on no other occasion to the same degree.[1] So it is; but it is the greatness not of the conquering hero, but of the hero who, although bleeding already from a hundred wounds, strikes his most powerful blow while the deadly shaft is piercing a vital organ. Mirabeau furnished incontestable proof on the 1st of March, that the Jacobins had not intimidated him on the previous evening, but he soon again ceased to attend their meetings.[2] Now, as

[1] Œuvres, V. 307.

[2] There is no reason to doubt that Lucas Montigny's statement to this effect is in the main correct, though he is mistaken in asserting that he never again set his foot into their hall. He had left it on the 28th saying: "I shall stay among you until I am ostracized," and from a letter of March 4th to La Marck we learn that he had been again at the club. But he reports a defeat: it is true, a defeat without a combat, for the scene which "les a remontés au diapason de la fureur" was enacted after he had left, but still a defeat. "Je suis en vérité très-découragé, très-embarassé, très-fâché de m'être mis si seul en avant, puisque tous les coups de la tempête vont porter sur le seul homme qui veuille la chose pour elle, et qui ne soit pas un hanneton."—Cor-

ever before, he took his stand on the stern facts.
As his turning himself into a Jacobin of the genuine dye was out of the question, he never again could exercise any influence there, and there was a fearful amount of truth in what Lameth had said: "Only from the midst of this Society can Mirabeau wield the lever of opinion;[1] outside of it all his force is of no use to him; as despised as Maury he becomes as powerless (*nul*)."[2] More and more the Jacobins succeeded in monopolizing the manufacture of popularity, and the ingredients of the article fabricated by them were unreason and everything antagonistic to true liberty. Mirabeau himself broke and tore the roots of his popularity by persisting in the attempt to force them into the double rock of reason and genuine liberty.

And by doing this he does not add a single grain to his influence with the court. Only a week after this terrible hand-to-hand struggle with the Radicals, Count Fersen, the gallant Swedish

resp., III. 78.—Laporte, intendant of the civil list, assures the king, March 3d, that Mirabeau's breach with the Jacobins is irreparable. Stern. II. 294.

[1] Mirabeau's rejoining the club in the beginning of October, after having stayed away from it for many months, was in itself an acknowledgment that there was a great deal of truth in the assertion.

[2] Aulard, II. 107, 108

knight of Marie Antoinette, writes to his sovereign, Gustavus III.: "His principles are always bad, but they are less so than those of the others. In spite of that, it is interesting not to have him against one." That is all the court cares for: not to have him for an open adversary. And thus one feels and thinks about him, although one is fully aware that, as Fersen expressly states, "he is compelled to hide himself under the forms of democracy in order not to lose all his influence." [1]

The part he had played in the revolution, as he wrote to Lafayette in April, 1790, rendered it impossible to him ever to be "neutral;" too many eyes were fixed upon him ever to admit of his hiding; with him even "silence" was sure to be counted "a crime." [2] And while he is thus forced, by his very superiority, always to fight in the forefront, every defeat he suffers, every unequal contest that, thanks to the valor of his arm, ends in a drawn battle, nay, every victory he achieves, ultimately tends to isolate him more and more. Higher and higher he towers above all the rest, but on the right and on the left they equally fall away from him. He knew well what that signified,

[1] March 8, 1791. Klinkowstroem, Le Comte de Fersen et la Cour de France, I. 86.   [2] Corresp., II., 3.

for he did not—complacently or cowardly—shut his eyes against the facts when they boded no good to him personally. This constantly progressing isolation meant that his every step was a step further to the brink of the Tarpeian rock, for in contending for the salvation of France he was contending against an irreversible decree of fate —not that inscrutable arbitrary power of the ancients, but simply the necessary resultant of the unalterable given facts. No mortal has ever issued as victor from such a contest. Therefore nothing better could have befallen him, than that he was called off on the 2d of April after an illness of but a few days. Up to this day many have thought differently. More than one eminent historian has declared it an open question whether he could have reversed the wheels. Why have they not gone to Mirabeau himself for an answer to their question? He has given it often and plainly enough. What he had told the king in his letter of the 10th of May, he had repeated in a different form, but fully as emphatically in his Note of December 4th: "One can count upon my zeal, but not on an omnipotence which I do not have."[1] To arrest, single-handed, the downward

[1] Corresp., II. 383.

course of the revolution required nothing less than omnipotence.

One of the unalterable facts of no small moment was Mirabeau's own past. No one knew better than he the tremendous weight of the chain that was thereby riveted to his wrists. Already in the fall of 1789, he often bitterly exclaimed in the hearing of La Marck: "Oh, what harm the immorality of my youth does to the public cause!" We have heard him repeatedly declare that character is the paramount requisite for a statesman, and that he—and he alone—possessed it. The first assertion is incontestable, and the second was true as to courage and force of will. But there is a third element indispensable in the make-up of a genuine statesman's character. The motives and the ends must be essentially moral. Was Mirabeau possessed of this requisite? Could it be presumed that he possessed it? It was this question that rendered his past an almost insurmountable barrier between him and success. Confidence he needed above all, and just this he found nowhere. It was bitter and cruel, but terribly true what the father had written: "He gathers in what those reap who have failed as to the basis, the morals... He will never obtain confidence, even if he tried to deserve it."[1]

And it was by no means only the immorality of his youth that caused all to distrust him. The kind of double game which the uncontrollable circumstances forced upon him, necessarily furnished always fresh aliment to the distrust of all. But there is no denying, that from first to last he also added fuel to the fire, when he would not have needed to do so and even might have damped it. Immorality was so deeply ingrained into his whole being, that it would crop out at the slightest provocation or temptation. Turn and twist as we will, there is as to state affairs—and especially in

[1] Loménie, IV. 141. In 1785 Mirabeau had written in his answer to Beaumarchais : "Mon premier but, en me vouant à la perilleuse profession d'apôtre de la vérité, fut de mériter l'oubli de mes longues erreurs. Voilà le seul intérêt, la seule ambition que je connus jamais : et j'espère en obtenir le succès : car enfin qu'importent au public les écarts d'une folle jeunesse, si l'âge mûr lui paie un tribut noble et généreux ? Mais malheur à ceux qui se feraient un titre de torts dès long-temps avoués, cruellement expiés, et peut-être suffisamment réparés, pour me refuser les égards que mérite tout citoyen incessamment occupé d'études, de recherches, d'ouvrages qui intéressent le bien général !"—Mémoires, IV. 276, 277. This time the father proved to be the better prophet.—In a letter to Soufflot (Oct. 4, 1787), Mirabeau says : "Les folies d'une bouillante jeunesse, ont été le premier aiguillon qui m'a pressé de payer à mon pays un tribut noble et généreux."—Mem., IV. 449.

great revolutionary upheavals—some truth in his maxim, that "the petty morality kills the great morality." But he put a strong dose of cynicism into it and was ever lamentably ready to make it a cloak for his inexcusable moral trippings. Thereby he to the last continues to be his own worst enemy. While his right breaks one link of the chain dragging down his arm, the left is busy putting a fresh rivet to another or forging a new one. He is an assiduous ally of cruel fate, denying him the possibility of applying to their full extent the extraordinary powers bestowed upon him by nature.

And yet it surely might have been different. The moral pollution was certainly not only skin-deep. The whole blood was vitiated. But in the depths of this Titanic character lay a vast moral reserve force.[1] It was doomed to remain latent,

[1] La Marck, telling of his offer to aid him in his pecuniary embarrassments in order to put him "en état de conserver son indépendence et de ne s'occuper que du bien public et de sa gloire," writes: "Il fut profondément touché de ma sollicitude pour sa gloire, et l'éloquence naturelle, mais entraînante, avec laquelle il me peignit son émotion, me confirma de plus en plus dans la conviction qu'il y avait de puissantes ressources dans le cœur d'un tel homme. . . Dans plusieurs circonstances, lorsque je fus irrité de son language révolutionnaire à la tribune, je m'emportai contre lui avec beaucoup d'humeur. . . je l'ai vu alors répandre des larmes

but the two magic words, Possibility and Responsibility, might have brought it into full activity at any moment. Nothing less than a task commensurate to his ambition and to his powers could bring his great and good qualities into full play, and nothing less than the full weight of supreme official responsibility could keep him steady. But by this stimulus combined with this ballast, what was weak and vile in him would have been brought so far under control, that he would have become what he could be. For the weak and the vile were in the main but acquired qualities, a volcanic temperament, miseducation, the follies, vices, and crimes of a rotten political system and a rotten society, and a tangle of untoward accidental circumstances concurring in planting the germs and nursing them into luxuriant growth. The great and good were inborn and therefore ineradicable, though dross be piled ever so high over them. Nature had made an uncommon effort in moulding this man, and life had made an uncommon and

comme un enfant, et exprimer sans bassesse son repentir avec une sincérité sur laquelle on ne se pouvait tromper. Il faut avoir eu avec un pareil homme des relations aussi suivies et aussi intimes que les miennes, pour connaître tout ce que la pensée a de plus élevé et le cœur de plus attachant."—Corresp., I. 108, 109.

most persistent effort to corrupt nature's masterwork. There was but one incentive powerful enough to arouse him to the supreme effort required for terminating the contest between nature and life by a glorious victory of the former: by putting him to the highest test, in allowing him to contend for the highest prize, he could be induced to conquer himself.

He knew it, for he said so. In the Note of June 20th, he charges the queen to tell Lafayette: "He needs a great aim, a great danger, great means, a great glory."[1] There is nothing "inexplicable" about him, if one but grasps the tremendous import of these words, and sees that they are the main key to his character. What an awful pathos they impart to his whole career! Yes, he *needs* a great aim and a great glory. His becoming *truly* great depends on having a chance accorded him to be *very* great. It was denied him, and a life which nature had intended to become an enduring blessing and the glory of a great nation, was rendered but a tragical incident in its history, bearing no fruit and leaving no trace. What Mirabeau had been foremost in destroying and what had to be destroyed, would have

[1] Corresp., II. 42.

crumbled into dust though he had never lived. As to the positive tasks confronting France, he, however, was "the party of one man." He alone was able to construct *pari passu* with the destroying, and thus to construct, that the new structure would be adapted to the true nature and actual condition of things. But he was condemned to spend all his forces in checking and abating as to this or that detail, the blunders of all the rest, in numberless cases amounting, as to their effects, to irredeemable crimes. Not enough that doctrinarianism and prejudice, indolence and passion, obtuseness and perversity prevent him from arresting the universal pressing on towards chaos and anarchy; his very devices for doing so are perverted into battering-rams for breaking down the last bulwarks, and more than once he is compelled to assist the madmen himself. Never had France stood in greater need of a pre-eminent, constructive statesman, never had she had to boast of a greater political genius, never had a statesman yearned more ardently to rescue her, though it cost the last drop of his heart's blood, and—as he himself said—he had only pre-eminently contributed to a vast destruction, which, as he predicted again and again, would irresistibly go on so long as anything was left to be destroyed. That was an infinitely more tragical fate than that of being assassinated like Cæsar for being too great, or that of suffering like Louis XVI. a felon's death, at the hands of an ungrateful people for having been too small.

As early as January, 1790, Mirabeau bitterly complained: "Always restricted to advise, never able to act," I shall probably have the fate of Cassandra: "I shall always predict truly, and shall never be believed." [1] Like all his prophecies, the prediction was fulfilled to the letter. Nor would he have escaped this sad fate, if there had been no taint upon his character. "Falling myself, and probably one of the first, under the sickle of fate," he writes in his Note of August 17th, "I shall be a memorable example of what is reserved to men that are, in politics, ahead of their contemporaries." [2] Yes, his being ahead of his times was the primary and principal cause why all his construc-

[1] Corresp., I. 449.
[2] Corresp., II. 138. It is interesting to note in this connection La Marck's opinion, that Mirabeau would " unquestionably " have ended on the guillotine, if he had not died a natural death, ere Master Samson, the executioner of Paris, became the greatest equalizer of France. Of Mirabeau's determination " de sauver le roi dans le bouleversement général, et de l'arracher aux mains des anarchistes, qui ne pouvaient pas manquer de devenir bientôt ses bourreaux," LaMarck says: " C'était risquer sa vie."—Ib., I. 151, 152.

tive political genius[1] could bear no other fruit than dismal prophecies, which stand unparalleled in truthfulness and unerring minuteness.

When his supreme hour had come the distant boom of cannon drew from him the proud question: "Are these already the funeral rites of Achilles?" And one of his last words was: "I take with me the shroud of the monarchy; after my death the factions will fight over its shreds." So they did, becoming more and more convinced, that to demolish not only royalty, but government, was to establish liberty. The mortal remains of Mirabeau were the first to be deposited in the Pantheon, which the National Assembly consecrated to the ashes of the greatest sons of France. When that revolutionary version of the gospel of liberty had attained full sway, they were cast out and those of Paul Marat, who had demanded the highest gallows for him, put in their place; where they now mingle with the dust, nobody knows nor ever will know. Thus the Terrorists were the last to confer a mark of honor upon him. For

[1] To obtain an adequate idea of Mirabeau's fertility in positive and constructive ideas, it is indispensable to consult those also of his writings, which most of his biographers have not deemed worthy of any attention. See for instance the *Mémoires*, IV. 91–104.

who will deny that it was an honor, even in the coffin, to be ostracized by those who made terror the foundation of liberty, canonized the guillotine, and kicked God Almighty out of His temples to make room for the goddess of Reason. Most of those who had done the best to bring this about, learned how holy the guillotine was when they were made to ascend its fatal steps themselves. Those who survived saw the red cap of Liberty expand and stiffen into a military cocked hat. Even in the first year of the revolution Cassandra—Mirabeau had foretold this transformation as explicitly as the end of the king and the queen. Is eloquence a source whence such predictions can spring? The French historians have read and registered these and all his other prophecies, verified by the facts, but with most of them, the superabundance of a whole century's stern lessons have not sufficed to open their eyes to the fact that his claim to greatness cannot chiefly rest upon his oratory. He himself declared, in so many words, that in his own estimation he was, above all, statesman, and only in the second place orator and writer.[1] In quantity and in quality, the work done by France since the establishment of the third

[1] Aug. 26, 1790, to La Marck. Corresp., II. 146.

republic in regard to the history of the revolution challenges the highest admiration. Is it nevertheless to last another century ere she is prepared to do full justice to her greatest son of the greatest period of her history? Who can tell? Mere knowledge of the facts does not suffice. Her judgment upon this chapter of her past must be warped so long as she flinches from probing the present to the quick; and much as the third republic has done for the intellectual and political advancement of the nation, it has as yet not produced that supreme moral courage required by the precept of the Greek sage: " Know thyself!"

THE END.

INDEX.

Aix, Mirabeau's suit against his wife at, 216.
American war, effects of, 101.
Ancien Régime, political structure under, 2 ff. ; system of justice under, 6, 211 ; self-government under, 13 ; over-government under, 14 ; sale of offices under, 15 ; financial embarrassments under, 19 ; estate under, 20; clergy, 20 ff. ; nobility, 26 ff. ; destroys itself, 124 ; utter bankruptcy, 126 f. ; many-headed opposition to, 129 ff. ; destroyed by Louis XIV., 132 ; has disintegrated people, 152 ; inconsistency of, 210 f.
Archives Parlementaires, II. 108, 109 ; confusion as to Blin's speech, II. 112 (note).
Army, practically dissolved, II. 152 ; Mirabeau proposes reorganization, II. 153.
Arneth, 74 (note) ; 78 (note) ; 90 (note).
Arnold, Matthew, 75.
Assignats, II. 161 ff.
Attroupements, bill against, II. 67 ; II. 84.

Bachaumont, on the economists, 148 ; on Rousseau's Contrat Social, 158.
Bacon, II. 212 and note.
Banque de Saint Charles, denunciated by Mirabeau, II. 172.
Bar, 156 (note).
Barante, on optimism, 237.

Barentin, opening speech, 243.
Bastille, stormed, II. 21 ; effects of storming of, II. 42.
Beaumarchais, Mirabeau's letter to, II. 237 (note)
Berthier, murdered, II. 23.
Besançon, intendant of, on sentiment in his province, 239.
Besenval, opinion of M. Antoinette, 87 (note) ; testifies as to elasticity of marriage bond, 181 (note).
Blanc Louis, on Mirabeau's position in Assembly, II. 7.
Blin, speech against Mirabeau, II. 110.
Bouillé, on nobility, 27 ; on financial ruin of nobility, 67, 232 ; conduct at Nancy, II. 152.
Bourgeoisie, apish vanity of, 43 ; attitude toward proletariat, 51 f ; Robespierre against, 53 ; disintegration of, during rev., 55 ; improving material conditions of, 56 ; intellectual conditions under *anc. rég.*, 56 ; engage in discussion of polit. problems, 150.
Brienne, 116 ; dismisses notables, 116 ; is dismissed, 125.
Buffière, Pierre, name of Mirabeau at school, 195.

CABANIS, quotes Mirabeau as to action after flight of king, II. 185.
Café Foy, resolutions of, II. 45 (note).
Caisse nationale, suggested by Mirabeau, II. 103.
Calonne, on penalties from *gabelle*, 37, 103 ; appointed *contrôleur général*, 106 ; his *début*, 107 ; his financial policy, 107 ff ; takes up Turgot's reform programme, 109 ; has assembly of notables called, 110.
Campan, Mme, on appointment of Maurepas, 90 (note).
Cassagnac, 112 (note).
Champford, 77 (note).
Chapellier, proposes committee on emigration, II. 224.
Chatelet, Marquise du, treatment of *canaille*, 52.
Choquard, Abbé, one of Mirabeau's teachers, 195.
Christianity, seriously undermined, 136.
Church, s. clergy ; intolerance, 133 ff ; loses religious content, 136 ; merely privileged class, 136.

Cicé (archbishop), acts as go-between for Mirabeau and Lafayette. II. 87; intrigues against Mirabeau on Nov. 7, II. 118.
Clement XI., 133.
Clergy, taxes levied by, 22 f; upper and lower, 23 f; riches of, 23 and note; poverty of lower, 24; luxury of higher, 24; delusions of rev. leaders about, 25.
Clergy of France, 20; form of contribution to state, 21; conditions attached to grants by Ordinary Assembly of, 22; political activity of, 22.
Clugny, 96.
Colbert, 101.
Compte rendu, 103; limitations of, 104; political importance of, 105; success of, 106.
Condorcet, delusion about the nature of man, 158.
Conseil du roi, 10.
Contrôleur général, 11.
Constitution, to be made, 253 ff; untoward conditions for making of, 257 f.
Corvée, 35; abolished, 94; re-established, 98.
Cour plénière, 122.
Courrier de Provence, II. 22; II. 46; II. 84; II. 86.
Court, s. Versailles and nobility; d'Argenson on, 72; charm of, 74 ff.
Croupes, 71.

D'AIGUILLON, Mirabeau refused admission at, II. 226.
Daire, 102 (note).
D'Antraigues, Mirabeau praises moderation to, 236.
D'Aragon, Marquise (Mirabeau's niece), II. 87.
D'Argenson, on court, 72; on study of public law, 143; on anti-monarchical opposition, 145.
De Biauzat, Gaulthier, II. 149.
De Castries, II. 148.
December Memoir, II. 188 ff.
De Fleury, 106.

250   INDEX.

De Lamoignon (Guillaume), view of power of States-General, 220.
De la Tour, on optimism, 237, 238.
De Pailly (Mme.), becomes Marquis Mirabeau's mistress, 184; character, 185; as a mischief-maker, 185.
Desmoulins, Camille, praise of mob-rule, 256; judgment on 5th of Oct., II. 41; on necessity of lying, II. 50 (note); II. 53; describes insurrection of women, II. 55 f.; on Lafayette, II. 59; describes attack at Jacobin club on Mirabeau, II. 227 f.
Despotism, Essay on, s. Mirabeau, 212.
D'Esprémenil, 119 (note).
D'Estaing, Louis' letter to, II. 51 and note; II. 64.
Dictionnaire philosophique, 147.
Dohm, on Mirabeau's mastery of art of asking, II. 210.
Don gratuit, 21; voted by Ordinary Assembly, 21.
D'Ormesson, 106.
Droz, quoted, II. 217.
Dubarry, Madame, 88.
Dumont, assertion concerning connection of Mirabeau with *Monsieur*, II. 174 (note).
Dupont de Nemours, 109.
Duport, 11. 227 f.
Duroveray, II. 149.

ECONOMISTS, 147; a sect, 148.
Edict of Nantes, revocation of, 132.
Elliott, Grace D., on Duke of Orleans' share in events of Oct., II. 61 (note).
Estates, character of two upper, 20; privileges of, 20; first estate, 20 f; second estate, 26.
Etats Généraux, published by Mirabeau, II. 18; suppressed, II. 18.
Etiquette, of Versailles, 64 ff.; as to money-affairs, 67, 68.

FEDERATION FESTIVAL, II. 5.
Fersen, Count, on Mirabeau, II. 234.

INDEX. 251

Feudalism, in France and Germany, 29 ; in France, 29 f. ; shattered, II. 24.
Fifth of October, Lecture VIII. ; origin of insurrection of, II. 47 ff. ; a well-laid plot, II. 55 ; effects of, II. 65.
Finances, under *anc. rég.*, 19 ; embarrassments because of, 19 ; example of bankruptcy of court, 69 ; Necker at head of, 100.
Flour-war, 97.
Foreign clergy, 21 (note).
Form, as first law of life, 74 ff. ; drawback of, 76.
Fourth of August, called an "orgy," II. 24.
France, *ancien régime* (which see) ; resources of, 19 ; attitude toward Mirabeau, 258 ; fails to appreciate Mirabeau, II. 244 f.
François (baker), murdered, II. 84.
Frederick the Great, absolutism compared with that of Versailles, 63 ; again, 72.
Frederick William, 72.
French idealism, 258.
French literature of 18th century, not a cause but a symptom, 142 ff. ; is revolution in abstract, 152.
Frochot, II. 139.

Gabelle, 36 ; penalties from, 32.
Généralité, 11.
Government, abject senility of, 125 ; drove intellect into opposition, 131 ; logical outcome of insistence on *per capita* vote, 247 ; abdicates to States-General, 248, 257 ; II. 43 f.
Grands bailliages, 122.
Grimm, rosy view of future, 151 (note); on prevalence of speculation, 162.
Guilds, 47 f.; proletariat formed by, 48.

HÆUSSER, Ludwig, II. 30.
Hamilton, Alexander, on nature of Man, 157.

Holland, T. E., 156 (note).
Hôtel de Ville, mob cleared out of, II. 62.
Huguenots, Turgot's exertions in behalf of, 134.

INTENDANT, 11.

JACOBIN CLUB, Mirabeau president of, II. 208, 220; Mirabeau attacked at, II. 227 ff.
Jansenism, 133.
Jefferson, on king, 95; on notables, 112; on Lafayette, II. 140.
Jesuits, suppressed, 135.
Joseph II., letter on French government, 73 (note); criticism of French society, 77 (note).
Journal historique, 93 (note).
Joux, Fort, 202.

KAPP, 206 (note).

LA FARE, on nature of privileges, 227 f.
La Marck, 75; on composition of States-General, 249 (note); II. 5; on Lafayette in Versailles, II. 63 f.; testifies to Mirabeau's innocence concerning Oct. events, II. 67, 68, 81; gives memoir of 15th Oct. to Count of Provence, II. 79; charges Cicé with defeat of Nov. 7th, II. 118; is charged with Mirabeau's defence, II. 167; acts as mediator between court and Mirabeau, II. 176; laments incompleteness of connection, II. 192 f.; on Louis XVI., II. 199; on Marie Antoinette, II. 202, 212; on necessity of intrigue, II. 221; on Mirabeau's moral character, II. 238 (note).
Lafayette, II. 8, 23; attitude on 5th Oct., II. 56, 58 ff.; lapses of memory in his " Recollections," II. 60; his treachery to Mirabeau, II. 126, 136; in Versailles, II. 63; history of attempted alliance with Mirabeau, II. 88 ff.; his polit. creed considered, II. 126 (note);

INDEX. 253

his great power after Oct. events, II. 133 ff. ; reasons
why he does not accept alliance with Mirabeau, II.
134 ff. ; his vanity, II. 138 ff. ; defeats Mirabeau's
ambition to be president during federation festival,
II. 138 f. ; his indecision, II. 143 ff. ; sources of power,
II. 145 ff. ; action in veto-question, II. 159 ; denies
Mirabeau's venality, II. 179.

Lally-Tollendal, II. 23.

Lameth. Alexandre, 124 (note); wounded in duel, II. 148 ;
attacks Mirabeau at Jacobins, II. 227 f. ;

Lamoignon, 114 (note).

Lanjuinais, speech against Mirabeau, II. 112.

Lantern, as means of execution, II. 56.

Law (financier), 103.

Le bailli, s. Le chevalier de Mirabeau.

Le Tellier (Jesuit), 133.

Lemontey, 131.

Lettres à Mauvillon, quoted in notes.

Lettres de cachet, 198, 199 ; work by Mirabeau on, 214.

Levrault, Mirabeau's letters to, II. 11.

Limousin, Turgot intendant of, 98 ;

Lit de justice, 9 ; of March, 1776, 94.

Louis XVI., slave of etiquette, 65 (note) ; education and
character, 84, 85 ; La Marck's opinion of, 85 (note) ;
expects great things of notables, 113 ; sees through
Parliament. 117 (note) ; on States-General in 1776,
120 (note) ; speech at opening of States-General, 240 ;
plays a passive part on 5th and 6th Oct., II. 51 ; during
6th Oct., II. 64 ; appoints ministers from Assembly,
II. 108 ; chargeable for failure of Mirabeau's plans,
II. 193 ; characterized by Montmorin and La Marck,
II. 198 f.

Louis XIV., maxim of *l'état c'est moi*, 3 ; sale of offices
under, 16 (note), 26 ; Versailles, creation of, 62 ;
prominence of court, 63 f. ; called *le roi soleil*, 64 ;
demoralization of France through, 71 ; hated by
people, 81 ; destroys *anc. rég.*, 132 ; his church policy.
132 f. ; results of church policy, 134.

Louis XV., principle of government, 3 ; as grain-speculator, 71 ; despised by people, 81 ; *après nous le déluge*, 82 and note.

Longo, Marquis, 172.

Loménie, 103 (note), 186 (note); on Mirabeau's education, 195; injustice of, 198, 199 ; calls Mirabeau "inexplicable," II. 2; criticism of work of, 2 ff. ; sees only orator in Mirabeau, II. 6 ; criticism of speech of Nov. 6th, II. 96 f. ; refutation of criticism of, II. 99 f. ; praises Mirabeau for conduct at Jacobins, II. 232.

Loustalot, II. 49 ; on preparations for 5th Oct., II. 55 (note), 57.

Louvois, 101.

Lowell, E. L., 13 (note) ; on feudal burdens, 29 ; on rural classes, 30 ; on material prosperity, 38.

Lying, in the revolution, II. 50.

MABLY, on danger of executive power, II. 36.

Malesherbes, 91, 105 (note).

Malouet, advice to Necker, 233 ; on Mirabeau's clearsightedness, II. 11 ; on interview with Mirabeau, II. 33, 66.

Manuel, 233 (note).

Marat, damns Mirabeau, II. 37 ; in Pantheon, II. 243.

Marie Antoinette, Mirabeau's favorable opinion of, 85 ; character of, 85 ff. ; Besenval's judgment on, 87 (note) ; contributes to Turgot's overthrow, 95 ; during 6th of Oct., II. 64 ; suspects Mirabeau, II. 81, 177 ; proposes to win Mirabeau, II. 177 ; Mirabeau calls her the one man at court, II. 200 ; no trust in Mirabeau, II. 201 ; characterized by La Marck, II. 202.

Marignane (Miss), marries Mirabeau, 200 ; character, 201 ; the *bailli's* opinion of, 201 (notes) ; her adultery, 202.

Marriage, character of, under *anc. rég.*, 180 f., 184, 204.

INDEX. 255

Masses, their condition, 238 f. ; attitude toward *bourgeoisie*, 239 ; support sought by Nat. Assembly, 254, 255 ; direct Nat. Assembly, 255.
Maupeou, 83.
Maurepas, 89 ; history of appointment, 89 (note) ; opposes Turgot, 92 ;
Mauvillon, II. 8 and note, 9, 26 (note); Mirabeau on his own moderation to, II. 27.
Méjan (editor of Mirabeau's speeches), 4 (note); II. 118.
Mémoir of 15th of October, its origin, II. 68 ; analysis of, II. 69 ff. ; its failure, II. 79 ; its penetrating insight, II. 79 f.
Mending, by government of Louis XVI., 83.
Mercure de France, II. 53.
Mercy d'Argenteau, 85 (note) ; assists in negotiations between court and Mirabeau, II. 176 ff., 192.
Mesdames (daughters of Louis XV.), table expenses, 69 ; influence appointment of Maurepas, 89 and note ; incident connected with their flight, II. 224 f.
Metra, on pol. inexperience of States-General, 250.
Mirabeau, Jean Antoine, in wars of Louis XIV., 167 ; Mirabeau genuine grandson of, 215.
Mirabeau, Victor Riquette, Marquis de, on agriculture, 31; on Paris, 61 ; prophesies as to result of Necker's system, 103 ; aversion to son, 164 ff. ; sows his wild oats, 169 ; settles down, 170 ; his economical labors, 170 ; his moralizing tendency, 170 f., 177 ; humanitarian, 171 ; believer in blue blood, 171 ; want of balance, 172, 173 ; devotion to mother, 172 ; son of *anc. rég.*, 174 ; sensitiveness, 175 (note); family ambition, 176 ; failure of speculations, 177 ; stubbornness, 178 ; *scribomania*, 179 ; paternalism, 180 ; marries, 180 f. ; takes a mistress, 184 ; guilt apportioned, 187; threatens to send son to Dutch colonies, 197 and note, 198 ; uses *lettres de cachet*, 199 ; requests to have Mirabeau locked up, 205 and note ; sends son to Vincennes, 207 ; reasons for releasing him, 208 ; tes-

tifics to son's oratory, 216; destroys his son's career, 218.

Mirabeau, chevalier de (*le bailli*), on Paris, 57 (note); on flour-war, 97 (note); most estimable character, 168; his wild youth, 168 and note; on his brother, 175 (note); on brother's speculations, 177; on Mme. de Pailly, 186 (note); on Mirabeau's wife, 201 (notes); on his brother's treatment of son, 209, 210 (note), II. 25; on his nephew's intelligence, II. 68.

Mirabeau, Marquise de, marriage, 180 f.; character, 182; adultery, 183; her lawsuit, 183; Mirabeau champions her cause, 205.

Mirabeau, 4, 10, 24 (note), 27; on Paris, 45; on money-favors of court, 70; under spell of form, 75; opinion of M. Antoinette, 85; reason for Calonne's failure, 109 (note); view of Calonne's end, 110; reason for joy at convocation of Notables, 113; claims to have advised convocation of Notables, 113 (note); on parliament, 117 (note), 118 and note; on necessity of summoning States-General, 126 (note); his birth, 164; sensuality, 182 and note; influence of household on, 188; father's treatment of, 189, 190 ff.; natural intelligence, 189, 190; charm exercised by, 192 and note; degraded to common rank, 195; in army, 197; nature of guilt, 197; tendency to contract debts, 200; marries, 200; falls in love with Sophie, 202; flight and sentence, 203 f.; his manner against his father, 205; at Vincennes, 206 f.; released, 207; tribute to his father, 208; sufferings at Vincennes, 210; essay on Despotism, 212; on *Lettres de Cachet*, 214; polit. importance of, 214, 217; announcement of pol. creed, 215; returns to prison voluntarily, 215; his oratory, 216; literary excellence of writings, 217; necessity of States-General, 234; joy over convocation, 235; his moderation, 236; his disgust with Necker, 236 f., 245; on Necker's speech, 241 f.; on inexperience of States-General, 250; on French national character, 251; on unwieldiness of Assembly, 252; on control of Assembly by masses, 255 ; II. 22, 46 ; on untoward conditions for making constitution, 257 ; is hissed, II. 1 ; selfishness not mainspring of activity, II. 4 f., 39 f. ; forms party of one man, II. 7 ; opinion of his own statesmanship, II. 8 (note) ; his practicality, II. 9, 10, 23, 24, 25 f., 31, 211 ; his programme, II. 11, 13, 17 f. ; his clear-sightedness, II. 12 ; on 23d of June, II. 14 f. ; on 4th of Aug. 24 f. ; his revolutionary spirit, II. 14 f. ; his royalism, II. 12, 29 ; his moderation, II. 17, 19, 27 f., 33 ; debate on assuming name of Nat. Assembly, II. 20 ; predicts despotism, II. 22 ; fears despotism of Assembly, II. 30 ; his foresight, II. 33, 35, 67, 79 ; his interview with Necker, II. 34 ; programme proposed to Montmorin, II. 34 f. ; insists on strong executive, II. 36 f., 66 ; his courage, II. 37, 38 f., 85 ; conduct on 5th and 6th Oct., II. 66 f. ; question of participation in Oct. events, II. 67 f., 80 f. ; Mémoir of the 15th Oct., II. 68 ff. ; his plan for salvation, II. 75 ff. ; his character, II. 83 f., 237 (note), 238 and note ; attempts to form alliance with Lafayette, II. 88 ff. ; is offered ambassadorship, II. 89 ; great speech of Nov. 6th., II. 96 ff. ; analysis of speech, II. 100 ff. ; considers means to establish concert between executive and legislative, II. 104 ff. ; moves to give ministers seat in Assembly, II. 108 ; his speech of the 7th, II. 113 ff. ; his defeat, II. 117 ; his noble patriotism, II. 119 and note, 121 ; on necessity of reconsidering decree of Nov. 7th, II. 120 f.; was he without a consistent policy ? II. 128 ff. ; absolute necessity of winning or destroying Lafayette, II. 133 ff. ; shares blame of defeat, II. 134 ; strictures on Lafayette, II. 142 ff. ; analyzes sources of Lafayette's power, I. 145 ; proposes to put Nat. Guard under order of king, II. 149 ; proposes reorganization of army, II. 153 ; attitude on question of peace and war, II. 154 f. ; attitude on question of royal veto, II. 158 f. ; attitude on question of *assignats*, II. 161 ff. ; attitude on church question, II. 165 ff. ;

17

measure of guilt for evil effects, II. 166 ; question of guilt of connection with court, II. 169 ; mitigating circumstances, II. 169 ff. ; carelessness about money, II. 171 f. ; is not venal, II. 172 f., 178 ; his connection with *Monsieur* after Nov. 7th, II. 174 f. ; history of connection with court, II. 176 ff. ; joy at overtures, II. 177 ; his profession of faith of May 10th, II. 178 f., 181 ff. ; the pecuniary agreement, II. 178 f. ; faithfulness to revolution and to king, II. 182 ff., 188 ff. ; deprived of influence on executive, II. 193 f. ; connection between him and Montmorin, II. 195 ; his ambiguous position, II. 197, 203 ff., 209, 214 ff., 219, 242 ; President of Jacobins, II. 208, 220 ; his means become less reputable, II. 220 ; President of Assembly, II. 223 ; defends right of emigration, II. 224 f. ; attacked at Jacobins, II. 227 ff. ; his death, II. 235, 243 ; the weight of his past, II. 236 f. ; personal causes of failure, II. 236 ff. ; constructive statesman, II. 241 ; suffers fate of Cassandra, II. 242 ; France unable to do justice to him, II. 244 f.

Mirabeau-Tonneau (younger brother of former), 172 (note).

Mirabeau's wife, s. Marignane.

Monnier, Sophie de, Mirabeau falls in love with, 202, 203 ; relations to husband, 203.

Monsieur, s. Provence, Count de.

Montesquieu, defends sale of offices, 17 (note); on Paris, 59.

Montigny, 172 (note); on Marquis Mirabeau, 179 ; II. 232 (note).

Montlosier, II. 87 ; speech against Mirabeau, II. 112.

Montmorin, 118 (note), 270 ; warned by Mirabeau, II. 32 f.; refuses to see Mirabeau, II. 34 ; connection between him and Mirabeau, II. 195 ; on Louis XVI., II. 198.

Morris, Gouverneur, on the French masses, 238 ; on Necker's opening speech, 241 : on Barentin's speech, 243 ; on reception given Mirabeau in Assembly, 259.

INDEX. 259

Mounier, leads deputation of women to king, II. 63; answer to Mirabeau, II. 66.

NAPOLEON, II. 79.

National Assembly, s. States-General; moderate character of, 242; wanting in practical statesmanship, II. 9, 117; does too much, II. 13 f.; prospective slavery of, II. 32; disagreement with Paris, II. 43; invaded by women, II. 62 f.; inconsistent course in question of interdependence between legislative and executive, II. 108 ff.; decrees itself infallible, II. 124; thanks Bouillé, II. 152; destroys executive, II. 155 ff.: adopts suspensive veto, II. 159; self-destructive effects, II. 160.

National Guard, is assurance of order. II. 44, 57, 58; Mirabeau's plan respecting, II. 149; compromise-measure adopted, II. 149; degeneration of, II. 150 f.

Necker, 18 (note), 19; at head of finances, 100; view of ability of, 100 f.; foolish policy, 101 ff.; reforms effected by, 103; his *compte rendu*, 103 ff.; dismissed, 106; reappointment of, 125; on proposed permanence of States-General, 229; leaves everything to haphazard, 230; has no programme, 233 f.; speech at opening of States-General, 241; effect of dismissal. II. 21; interview with Mirabeau, II. 34; judgment of Mirabeau on, II. 69; Oct. interview with Mirabeau, II. 92.

Nobility, 26 ff.; transformed into a privileged class, 26; character of lower, 26 f.; Mirabeau on. 27; higher, 27 f.; humanitarian spirit of, 31; position as class in state, 32 f.; no moral right to claim immunity, 32; direct and indirect taxation of, 33 f.; blue blood theory of, 41; petition of peers of 1717, 42; at Versailles, 65; wealth of. 67 (note): appeals to king for money, 68; offices created for, 69.

Notables, assembly of, 110; composition of, 110; Calonne's plan with regard to, 111; sarcastic reception of, 112; their single reform, 112; political importance of, 114.

Octroi, 54.
Oelsner, on Mirabeau's defence at Jacobins, II. 228.
Oncken, 94; doubts Mirabeau's sanity, II. 217 (note).
Optimism, epidemic, 237.
Orleans, Duke of, relation to events of Oct., II. 61 and note.

Palais Royal, II. 41; assists in regeneration of France, II. 45, 53.
Pantheon, Mirabeau's remains deposited in, II. 243.
Paris, Mirabeau on, 45, 58 (note); necessity of understanding, 45 f.; complex nature of, 46; masses of, 46 f.; view of *le bailli* on, 57 (note); upper orders in, 58; growth of, 59; ascendency of, 59; Montesquieu on, 59; Mirabeau's father on, 61; position criticised by Mirabeau, II. 71.
Parliaments, 8; character of legislative power, 8; origin of legislative power, 8 (note); crushed, 122; reply of Parliament of Toulouse, 122; claim to be representative, 144; of Rouen demands account of revenue, 145 (note); of Aix condemns a papal brief, 147.
Parliament of Paris, attitude toward guilds, 47: recalled from exile, 92, 93; later attitude, 116; opposition for its own sake, 117; escapes from exile by bargain, 119; its declaration of principle, 120; crushed, 122; sudden unpopularity of, 231.
Patriots, succeed economists, 149; their object, 149.
Pays d'état, 5.
Pays d'élection, 6.
Peasantry, condition of, 29 ff.; s. clergy and nobility.
Pensions, s. nobility; amount of, under Necker, 70.
Per capita, vote by, 243.
Philadelphia Convention, compared with Nat. Assembly, 253.

Philosophers, constituting opposition, 138 ; compared with reformers of 16th century, 138 ; leave one tenet of *anc. rég.* untouched, 142.
Philosophic spirit, s. philosophers ; in cabinet, 148 ; complete victory of, 152 ; does not base on fact, 153 ff.
Pierre-en-Cise, 211.
Place de Grève, II. 56.
Pompadour, Mme., 89.
Pontarlier, 202 ; Mirabeau returns to prison in, 215.
Portalis, pitted against Mirabeau at Aix, 216.
Press, liberty of, granted, 232.
Privileges, s. clergy and nobility ; moral disintegration caused by, 39, ff. ; consequences of destruction of, 44 ; in domain of labor, 47 ; upper orders cling to, 227 f. ; Mirabeau against, II. 11, 12.
Proletariat, 48, 49 ; pauperism of, 49 ; growing despair and lawlessness of, 50 f. ; becomes sovereign of France, II. 65.
Provence, Comte de, receives memoir of 15th Oct., II. 79 ; connection with Mirabeau, II. 174 and note.
Provence, claims to being a distinct "nation," 6 ; effect of hot sun of, 167.
Provinces, dependence on Paris, 60 ; Young's experience with, 60.
Public opinion, infallibility of, 141 ; Necker's tribute to, 141 (note).

QUESNAY, 170.

RABAUT SAINT ETIENNE, on possessions of nobility, 67 (note).
Reason, dominant, 139 ; dogmatism of, 140 ; defects of, 154.
Resources, s. France.
Republicanism, at court, 78 ; confused nature of, 79.

Revolutionary spirit, how far Mirabeau was identified with, II. 14.
Rights of man, discussion of, II. 23, 24.
Robespierre, on *bourgeoisie*, 53.
Rocquain, on recall of Parliament, 93 (note); on flour-war, 97 (note); on expulsion of Jesuits, 135, 137, 151.
Roland, Mme., epigram on liberty, 163.
Rosen, court duties of, 65.
Rouen, chosen as retreat for king, II. 76, 77.
Rousseau, 34; influence on society, 78; effect of writings on *bourgeoisie*, 150; on constitution of society, 153 and note; his doctrine of equality tested, 155 f.; his doctrine of man's nature considered, 157 f.; does not consider himself a *practical* statesman, 159; poison in teachings of, 160, 161.

SAILLANT, du, 208 (note).
Saillant, Mme. du (Mirabeau's sister), II. 119 (note).
Salons, engage in polit. discussion, 149.
Sansculottes, 53.
Séance royale, 120; of 23d of June, II. 14 f.
Séguier, 152 (note).
Ségur, on republicanism of society, 80.
Seven Years' War, effect of disasters of, 144.
Siéyès, on reign of terror, 55; on third estate, 57; on science of politics, 158; does not propose to put doctrines into practice, 159; rebuked by Mirabeau, II. 10.
Soulavie, 95 (note), 111 (note), 118 (note), 121 (note).
Spontaneous anarchy, 240.
St. Antoine, 52, 61.
St. Marceau, 52, 61.
St. Huruge, Marquis de, heads mob for Versailles, II. 44.
Staël (Mme. de) testimony as to repub. spirit of Paris, 150, 232 (note); repeats Necker's conversation with Mirabeau, II. 92; on Mirabeau, II. 214.
States-General, convened last in 1614, 41; term becomes popular, 119; inevitableness of, 126 and note; de-

INDEX. 263

manded by clergy, 137 ; negative import of, 219 ; belong to *anc. rég.*, 219 and note ; hist. views of power, 220 ; task assigned them by government, 221 ; indefiniteness of task, 221 ff. ; inevitable disagreement of, 224, 225 f. ; question of vote by orders discussed, 228 f. ; obstinate on vote *per capita*, 244 ff. ; composition of, 248; no political experience, 249 ff. ; want of unity of aim, 251 f. ; size, 252 ; bears character of constituent Assembly, 253, 256 ; situation at meeting of, II. 10 f. ; constituted Nat. Assembly, II. 20 f.

States-General (Holland), surrender Mirabeau, 206.

Stephens, H. M., on deputies to States-General, 248 ; on Mirabeau's statesmanship, II. 9.

Stock-jobbing, under Necker, 102.

Taille, 34.

Taille noble, 227.

Taine, on aristocracy before rev., 32 ; *en blocs* thinking of peasantry, 38, 39, 58 (note) ; on Versailles under *anc. rég.*, 62, 77 ; on revol. before revol., 151 ; on import of cry of return to nature, 153 ; "spontaneous anarchy," 240 ; II. 62 (note).

Talleyrand, 113.

Talon, II. 94 ; attempts to bring Lafayette to a decision, II. 95.

Taxes, inequality of, 20 ; method of levying, 35 ; inequality of province in regard to, 36.

Terray, 83, 117 (note).

Third estate, s. under clergy, nobility, and peasantry ; position toward other two, 41 ; demands recognition of equality, 227 ; double number of representatives, 230 and note.

Thouret, Mirabeau replies to, II. 30.

Tocqueville, view on centralization, 10 ; view on new provincial assemblies, 123 (note).

Toulon, murdered, II. 23, 38.

Troyes, parliament at, 119.
Turgot, on villages under *anc. rég.*, 12, 13; reforms in taxation, 36, 47; on selfishness of cities, 54; as *contrôleur général*, 91: opposition to, 91, 92; attitude toward exiled parliament, 92, and note; dismissed, 94, 95; his reforms annulled, 96; effect of dismissal, 98 f.; warns king against American war, 101 (note), 105 (note), 109; article, "*Fondation*," 148; optimist 237.

UNIGENITUS (bull), 133, 134.
United States, II. 103.

VAUVENARGUES, on Marquis Mirabeau, 179.
Vassan (Miss), marries Marquis Mirabeau, 180 f.
Versailles, focus of *ancien régime*, 62; ruins nobility, 67; mob starts for, II. 53 ff.
Vincennes (dungeon), 198, 207.
Voltaire, in Bastille, 42; *écrasez l'infame*, 138 (note); as apostle of reason, 140; predicts growing opposition of parliament, 144; article on grain, 147; on destructive spirit of philosophers, 163.
Von Gleichen, on Marquis Mirabeau's treatment of son, 191.
Von Sybel, 40.

WEBER, 114 (note); on Brienne's campaign against privileged orders, 232 (note).
Women, insurrection of, s. 5th of October.

YOUNG, ARTHUR, on activity of Paris, 60.

www.ingramcontent.com/pod-product-compliance
Lightning Source LLC
Chambersburg PA
CBHW031252250426
43672CB00029BA/2227